STAR WARS®

WORKBOOKS

2ND GRADE MATH

FOR AGES 7–8

BY THE EDITORS OF BRAIN QUEST
CONSULTING EDITOR: MICHAEL FLYNN

WORKMAN PUBLISHING
NEW YORK

Library of Congress Cataloging-in-Publication Data is available.

ISBN: 978-0-7611-7809-5

Workbook series design by Raquel Jaramillo
Cover illustration by Mike Sutfin
Interior illustrations by Lawrence Christmas

Workman books are available at special discounts when purchased in bulk for premiums and sales promotions as well as for fund-raising or educational use. Special editions or book excerpts can also be created to specification. For details, contact the Special Sales Director at the address below, or send an email to specialmarkets@workman.com.

Workman Publishing Co., Inc.
225 Varick Street
New York, NY 10014-4381

workman.com
starwars.com
starwarsworkbooks.com

Printed in the United States of America
First printing June 2014

10 9 8 7 6 5 4 3 2 1

STAR WARS®

WORKBOOKS

This workbook belongs to:

_____

Place Value Stars

You can use **place value** to figure out how much numerals are worth. Look at **32**:

tens ones

The **3** tells us there are **3 tens**.
The **2** tells us there are **2 ones**.

Look at the numerals and words below each card.

Write the number they equal on the line.

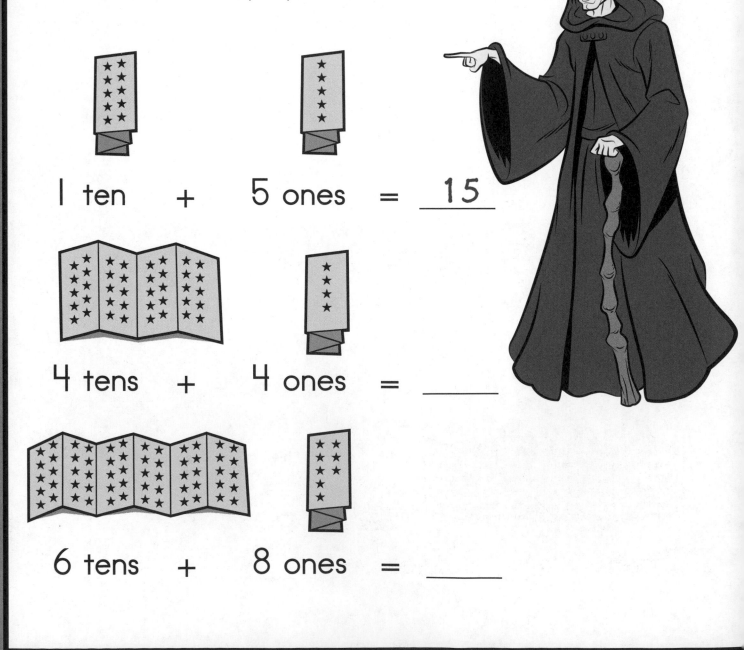

1 ten   +   5 ones   =   15

4 tens   +   4 ones   =   _____

6 tens   +   8 ones   =   _____

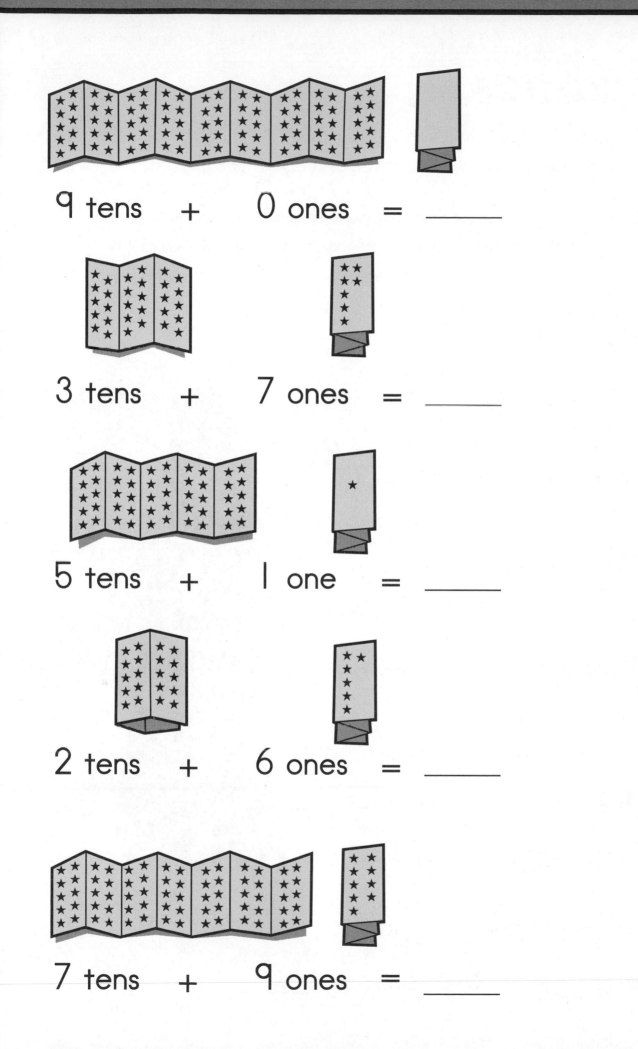

9 tens + 0 ones = _____

3 tens + 7 ones = _____

5 tens + 1 one = _____

2 tens + 6 ones = _____

7 tens + 9 ones = _____

Hundreds

If you see three numerals, you know that the number is made up of **hundreds**, **tens**, and **ones**. Look at **642**:

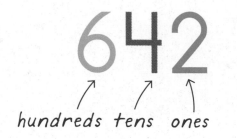

The **6** tells us there are **6 hundreds**.
The **4** tells us there are **4 tens**.
The **2** tells us there are **2 ones**.

Circle the correct numeral.

Circle the **ones**.   56③

Circle the **tens**.   84

Circle the **hundreds**.   125

Circle the **tens.**   368

Circle the **hundreds**.   620

Circle the **ones**.   56

Circle the **hundreds**.   157

Circle the **ones**.   917

Circles the **tens**.   586

Look at each number.

Then answer the questions.

275 How many hundreds? __2__ tens? __7__ ones? __5__

481 How many hundreds? _____ tens? _____ ones? _____

802 How many hundreds? _____ tens? _____ ones? _____

689 How many hundreds? _____ tens? _____ ones? _____

743 How many hundreds? _____ tens? _____ ones? _____

500 How many hundreds? _____ tens? _____ ones? _____

318 How many hundreds? _____ tens? _____ ones? _____

957 How many hundreds? _____ tens? _____ ones? _____

45 How many hundreds? _____ tens? _____ ones? _____

113 How many hundreds? _____ tens? _____ ones? _____

More Hundreds

Write the **place value** for each numeral on the chart.

	hundreds	tens	ones
426	4	2	6
193			
501			
978			
345			
109			
272			
486			
814			
768			
659			
321			

Draw a line to match the words to the number.

6 hundreds, 1 ten, 7 ones

3 hundreds, 2 tens, 8 ones

4 hundreds, 9 tens

2 hundreds, 5 tens, 2 ones

9 hundreds, 1 one

8 hundreds, 3 tens, 4 ones

7 ones

1 hundred, 7 tens, 3 ones

834

173

328

490

7

617

252

901

Words to Numbers

Draw a line to match the words to the number.

5 hundreds, 1 ten

8 tens, 8 ones

3 tens, 2 ones

1 hundred, 2 tens, 3 ones

7 hundreds, 1 one

2 hundreds, 8 tens, 5 ones

9 hundreds, 4 tens, 3 ones

32

285

943

701

510

123

88

Write out the number **529** using words:

_____

_____

Write the numbers on the sandcrawlers.

forty-seven

47

twenty-two

one hundred thirty-eight

three hundred twelve

seven hundred eighty-nine

six hundred eighteen

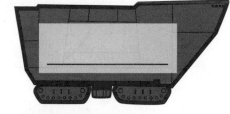

nine hundred two

My Numbers

Write how many of each you have in the chart.

Then answer the questions.

Parents	Siblings	Pets	Grand-parents	Aunts	Uncles	Wookiees

Which do you have the most of? _____

Least? _____

Are any the same number? _____

Complete the sentences with numbers.

Then write the numbers in words on the line.

I am _____ years old.

_____

I am _____ inches tall.

_____

I have _____ lightsabers.

_____

You're Invited!

The Ewoks are having a party for your birthday! Help them write the invitation by filling in the blanks.

Write the numbers in words.

_____
your name

will be _____ years old on
                    age

_____   _____
        month   day

Where: _____
                    street address

_____ , _____
        city   state

When: _____
                    date

At: _____
                    time

Compare the Candles

Write the number of candles beneath each birthday cake.
Then write **>** or **<** to show which cake has more candles.

< means **less than**.
> means **greater than**.

11   <   14

More or Less?

Write **>** or **<** to show which group has more clone troopers.

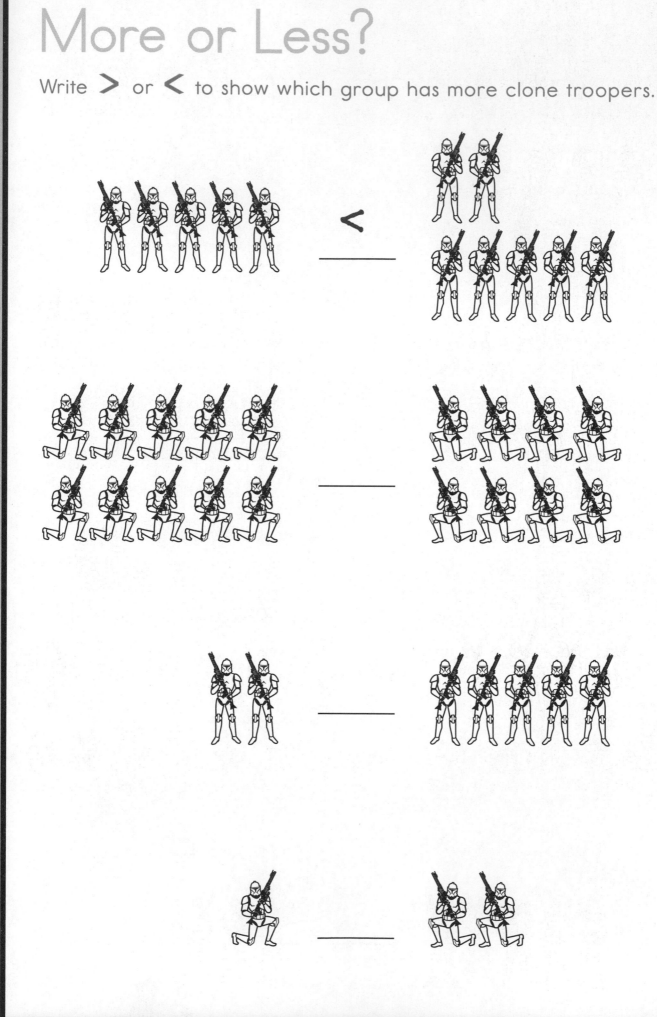

 _____

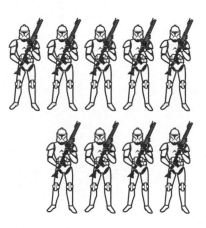 _____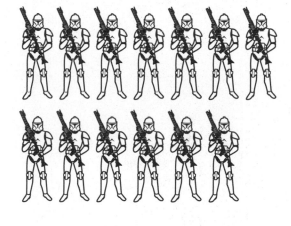

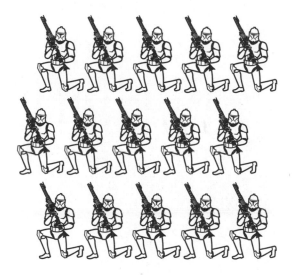 _____

 _____

Comparing Lightsabers

Compare the number of lightsabers.

Write **>** or **<** to show which group has more lightsabers.

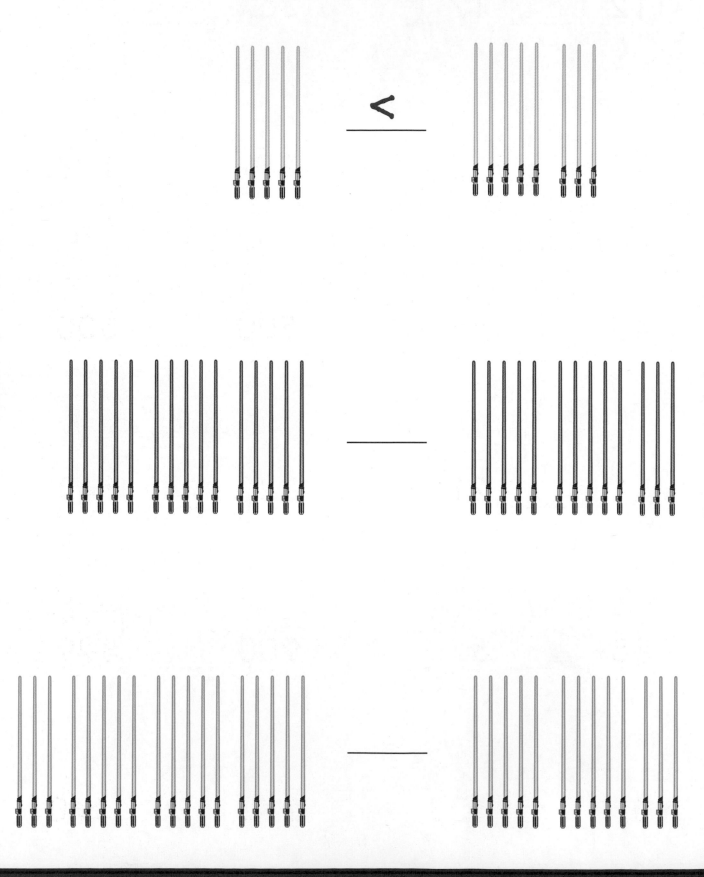

Write > or < to show which number is greater.

12 __<__ 17   364 _____ 346

98 _____ 100   289 _____ 198

45 _____ 65   500 _____ 600

11 _____ 21   823 _____ 843

88 _____ 8   900 _____ 899

102 _____ 103   240 _____ 340

Count by Twos!

Fill in the missing numbers in the smoke trail.

2

4

6

14

Count by Threes!

Fill in the missing numbers on the shipping containers.

3

___

___

___

15

___

___

Count by Fours!

Fill in the missing numbers in the bubbles.

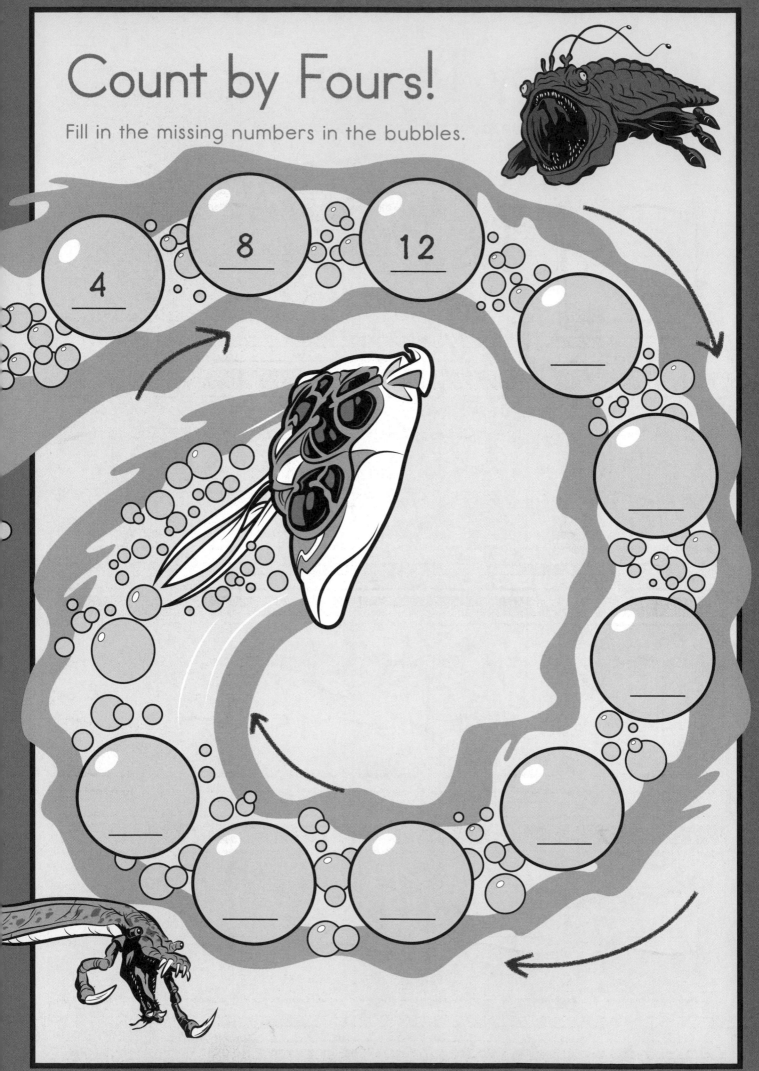

4

8

12

Count by Fives!

Fill in the missing numbers on the flags.

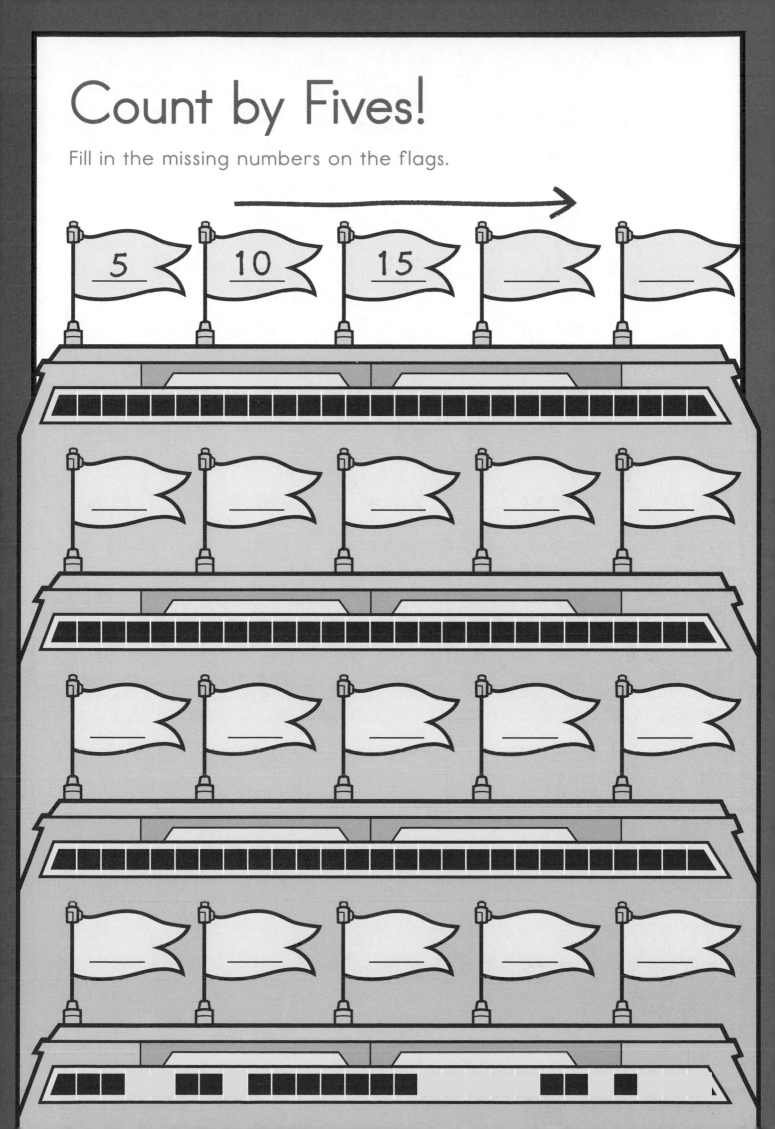

Count by Tens!

Fill in the missing numbers on the droids.

10   20   30

Count by Hundreds!

Fill in the missing numbers on the planets.

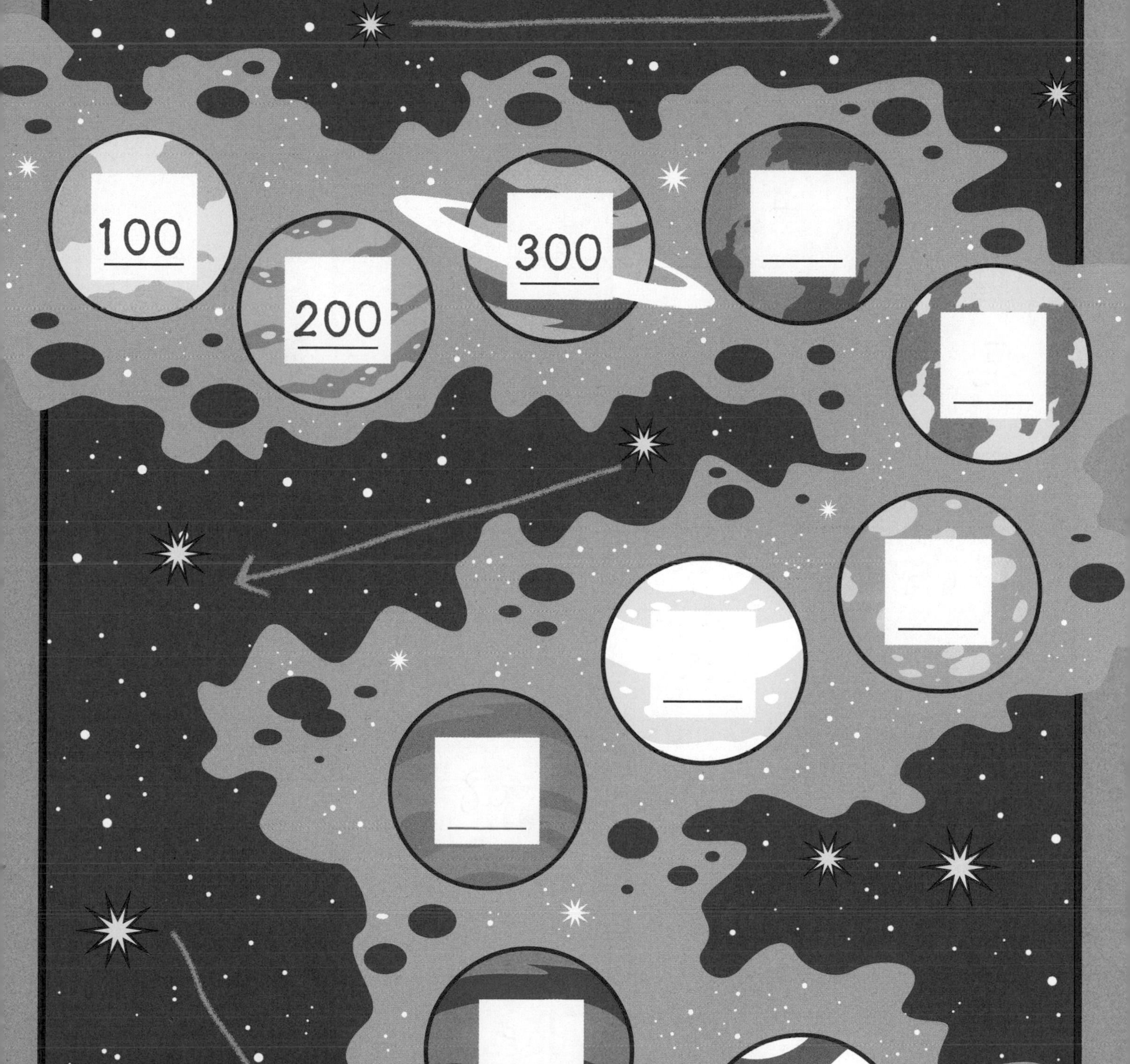

100

200

300

____

____

____

____

____

____

____

Odd or Even?

Count the droids on each card. Write the total in the yellow box.

Circle groups of 2 droids on each card.

If all the droids are circled, the number is **even**.
If there is a droid left over, the number is **odd**.

Color the cards with **even** numbers **blue**.

Color the cards with **odd** numbers **pink**.

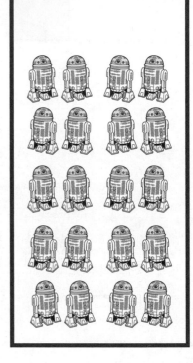

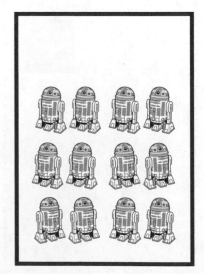

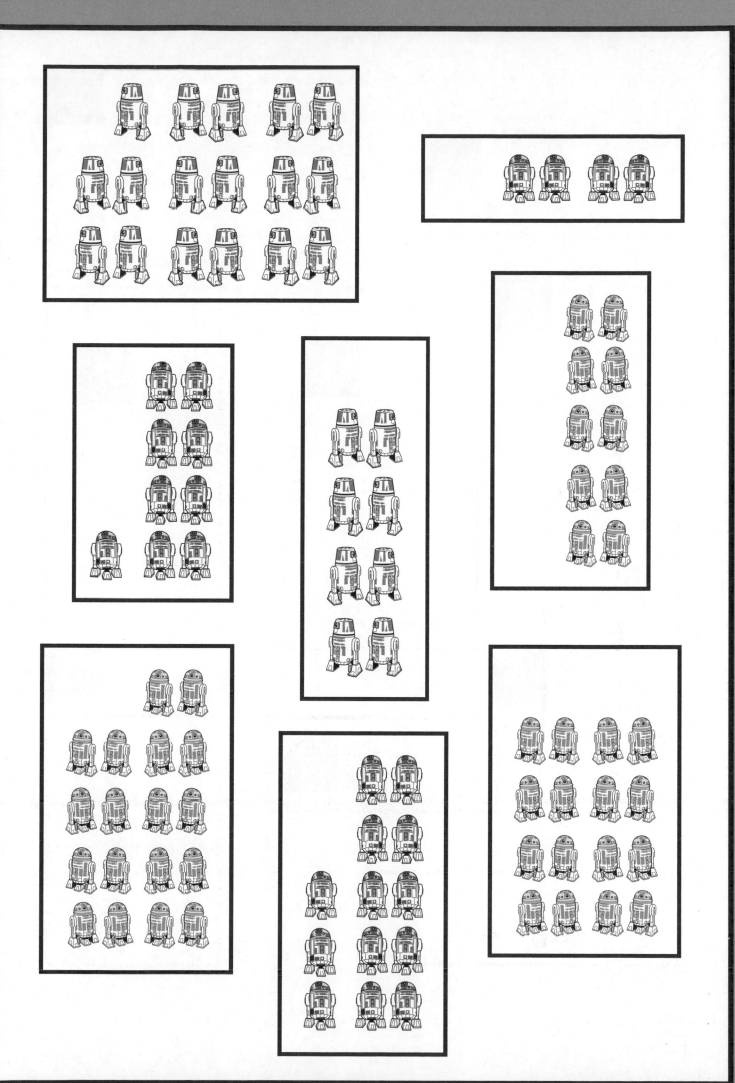

Sun Sums

Solve the equations on each sun.

If all the **sums** equal the number at the bottom, color the sun **yellow**.

If the **sums** do not equal the number at the bottom, color the sun **red**.

$7 + 2 =$ ___

$2 + 6 =$ ___

$4 + 4 =$ ___

$6 + 2 =$ ___

8

$5 + 5 =$ ___

$7 + 3 =$ ___

$2 + 8 =$ ___

$3 + 7 =$ ___

10

$4 + 0 =$ ___

$1 + 3 =$ ___

$2 + 2 =$ ___

$0 + 4 =$ ___

4

6 + 5 = _____

10 + 1 = _____

8 + 3 = _____

2 + 9 = _____

11

13 + 1 = _____

4 + 1 = _____

6 + 7 = _____

2 + 12 = _____

14

10 + 2 = _____

4 + 8 = _____

9 + 3 = _____

6 + 6 = _____

12

3 + 3 = _____

0 + 6 = _____

4 + 4 = _____

6 + 0 = _____

6

Add 10

Add. Write the **sum** on the line.

$$6 + 10 = \underline{\ 16\ }$$

$$10 + 10 = \underline{\ \ \ \ }$$

$$56 + 10 = \underline{\ \ \ \ }$$

$$33 + 10 = \underline{\ \ \ \ }$$

$$900 + 10 = \underline{\ \ \ \ }$$

124 + 10 = ____

157 + 10 = ____

235 + 10 = ____

868 + 10 = ____

544 + 10 = ____

667 + 10 = ____

212 + 10 = ____

345 + 10 = ____

Add 100

Add. Write the **sum** on the line.

100 + 100 = <u>200</u>

139 + 100 = ___

236 + 100 = ___

445 + 100 = ___

685 + 100 = ___

899 + 100 = ___

711 + 100 = ____

600 + 100 = ____

533 + 100 = ____

406 + 100 = ____

871 + 100 = ____

395 + 100 = ____

319 + 100 = ____

800 + 100 = ____

668 + 100 = ____

Tic-Tac-Total

Add each set of numbers. To win, draw a line through the three sums that are the same.

21 + 15	22 + 13	23 + 16
11 + 6	20 + 15	12 + 6
10 + 3	21 + 14	18 + 1

10 + 6	23 + 14	14 + 3
16 + 21	13 + 3	20 + 15
10 + 29	24 + 4	15 + 1

26 + 21	13 + 4	21 + 5
10 + 9	22 + 4	12 + 5
20 + 6	10 + 8	28 + 31

13 + 6	22 + 4	23 + 13
22 + 7	28 + 1	20 + 9
15 + 21	14 + 0	13 + 35

Cloud City Number Families

Addition facts can help you solve **subtraction** problems. It helps to think about **number families**.

All the **equations** in this family equal 6.

6

$4 + 2 = 6$ $2 + 4 = 6$

$6 - 2 = 4$ $6 - 4 = 2$

Finish the **number families**. Write the missing numbers.

12

$4 + 8 = \underline{12}$ $8 + \underline{} = 12$

$12 - \underline{} = 4$ $12 - 4 = \underline{}$

14

$5 + 9 = \underline{}$ $\underline{} + 5 = 14$

$14 - \underline{} = 5$ $14 - 5 = \underline{}$

13

$8 + \underline{} = 13$ $5 + 8 = \underline{}$

$13 - \underline{} = 8$ $13 - 8 = \underline{}$

16

$7 + 9 = \underline{}$ $9 + \underline{} = 16$

$16 - \underline{} = 7$ $16 - \underline{} = 9$

17

$7 + \underline{} = 17$ $10 + 7 = \underline{}$

$17 - 10 = \underline{}$ $17 - \underline{} = 10$

Lunar Subtraction

Solve the **equations** on each moon.

If all the **differences** equal the number in the yellow circles, color the moon **orange**.

If all the **differences** do not equal the number in the yellow circles, color the moon **blue**.

11 – 1 = _____

15 – 5 = _____

20 – 10 = _____

12 – 2 = _____

10

19 – 8 = _____

20 – 10 = _____

15 – 4 = _____

11 – 0 = _____

11

10 – 5 = _____

15 – 10 = _____

8 – 3 = _____

9 – 4 = _____

5

$16 - 0 =$ _____

$19 - 3 =$ _____

$18 - 2 =$ _____

$17 - 1 =$ _____

16

$12 - 0 =$ _____

$15 - 3 =$ _____

$13 - 1 =$ _____

$17 - 5 =$ _____

12

$10 - 2 =$ _____

$18 - 8 =$ _____

$12 - 2 =$ _____

$8 - 0 =$ _____

8

$1 - 0 =$ _____

$17 - 16 =$ _____

$2 - 1 =$ _____

$6 - 5 =$ _____

1

Subtract 10

Subtract. Write the **difference** on the line.

$$20 - 10 = \underline{\hphantom{0}10\hphantom{0}}$$

$$10 - 10 = \underline{\hphantom{000}}$$

$$34 - 10 = \underline{\hphantom{000}}$$

$$16 - 10 = \underline{\hphantom{000}}$$

$$595 - 10 = \underline{\hphantom{000}}$$

$$398 - 10 = \underline{\hphantom{000}}$$

$$110 - 10 = \underline{\qquad}$$

$$165 - 10 = \underline{\qquad}$$

$$390 - 10 = \underline{\qquad}$$

$$277 - 10 = \underline{\qquad}$$

$$817 - 10 = \underline{\qquad}$$

$$444 - 10 = \underline{\qquad}$$

$$880 - 10 = \underline{\qquad}$$

$$731 - 10 = \underline{\qquad}$$

$$695 - 10 = \underline{\qquad}$$

Subtract 100

Subtract. Write the **difference** on the line.

200 - 100 = _____

450 - 100 = _____

848 - 100 = _____

400 - 100 = _____

375 - 100 = _____

555 - 100 = _____

399 - 100 = _____

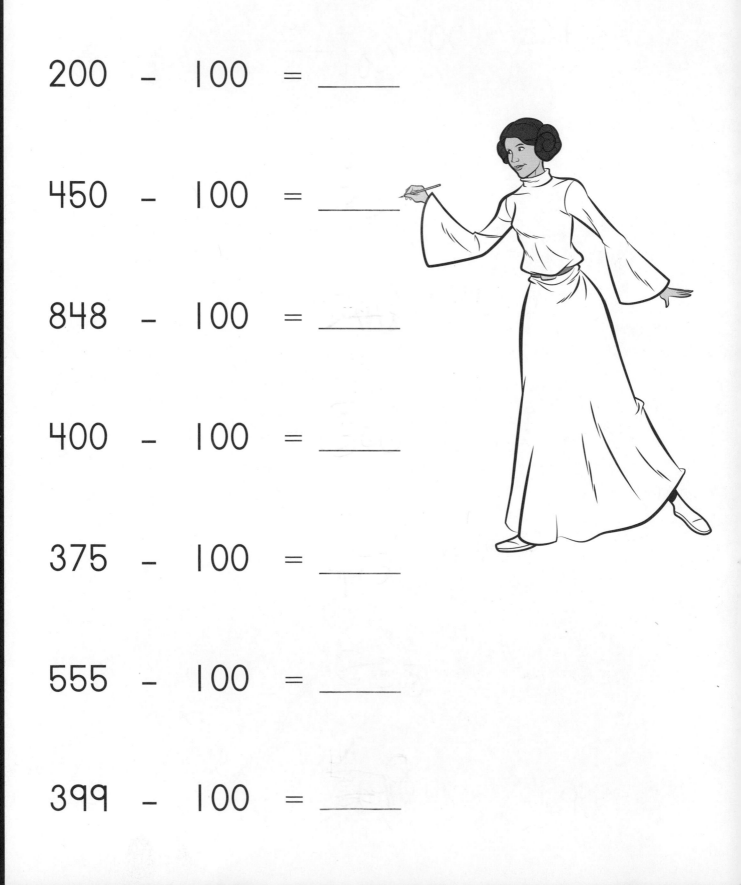

501 - 100 = _____

660 - 100 = _____

716 - 100 = _____

817 - 100 = _____

103 - 100 = _____

286 - 100 = _____

350 - 100 = _____

499 - 100 = _____

Tic-Subtract-Toe

Subtract each set of numbers. To win, draw a line through the three differences that are the same.

28 − 2	18 − 4	31 − 21
27 − 1	29 − 11	25 − 15
21 − 10	15 − 4	23 − 12

15 − 2	19 − 5	27 − 5
26 − 13	25 − 3	28 − 12
28 − 15	39 − 25	30 − 10

27 −20	26 −12	19 − 8
24 − 1	19 −12	29 − 18
27 − 11	24 − 12	38 − 31

23 −10	30 − 10	19 − 3
26 − 13	23 − 21	28 − 12
23 − 20	39 − 8	17 − 1

Colorful Surprise

Add or subtract. Then use the key to color the spaces.

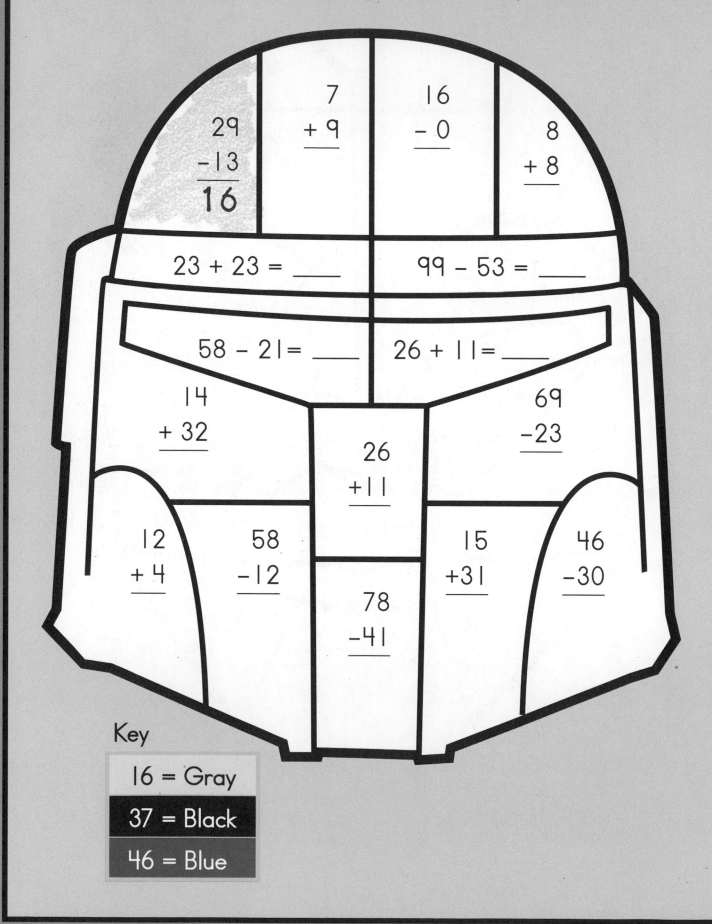

$$29$$
$$-13$$
$$\overline{16}$$

$$7$$
$$+9$$

$$16$$
$$-0$$

$$8$$
$$+8$$

$$23 + 23 = \underline{\quad}$$

$$99 - 53 = \underline{\quad}$$

$$58 - 21 = \underline{\quad}$$

$$26 + 11 = \underline{\quad}$$

$$14$$
$$+32$$

$$69$$
$$-23$$

$$26$$
$$+11$$

$$12$$
$$+4$$

$$58$$
$$-12$$

$$15$$
$$+31$$

$$46$$
$$-30$$

$$78$$
$$-41$$

Key

16 = Gray	
37 = Black	
46 = Blue	

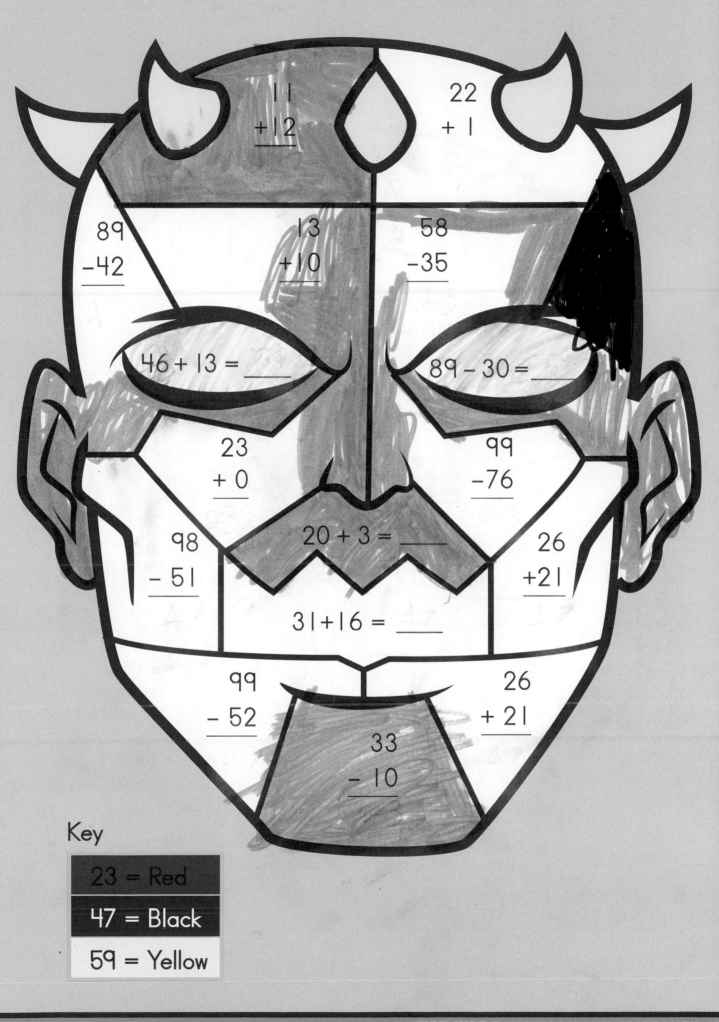

11
+12

22
+1

89
-42

13
+10

58
-35

46 + 13 = ____

89 - 30 = ____

23
+ 0

99
-76

98
- 51

20 + 3 = ____

26
+21

31+16 = ____

99
- 52

33
- 10

26
+ 21

Key

23 = Red
47 = Black
59 = Yellow

Break the Code

Add or **subtract**.

Use your answers to decode the riddle.

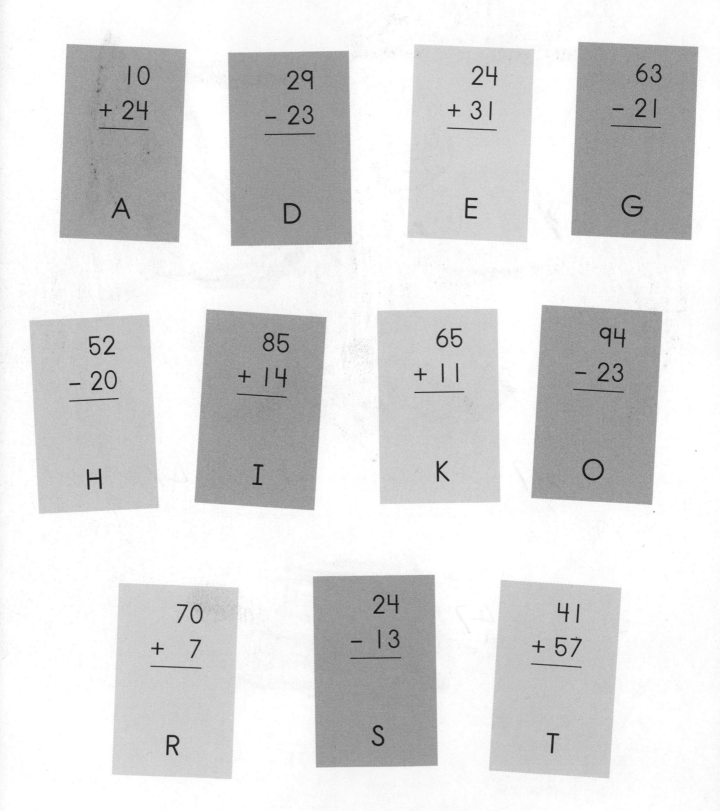

$$10 + 24$$ A

$$29 - 23$$ D

$$24 + 31$$ E

$$63 - 21$$ G

$$52 - 20$$ H

$$85 + 14$$ I

$$65 + 11$$ K

$$94 - 23$$ O

$$70 + 7$$ R

$$24 - 13$$ S

$$41 + 57$$ T

Riddle:

Why did Darth Vader cross the road?

Answer:

98	71		42	55	98		98	71		98	32	55
	6	34	77	76		11	99	6	55			

Luke's Dinner

Add or **subtract**.

Use your answers to decode the riddle.

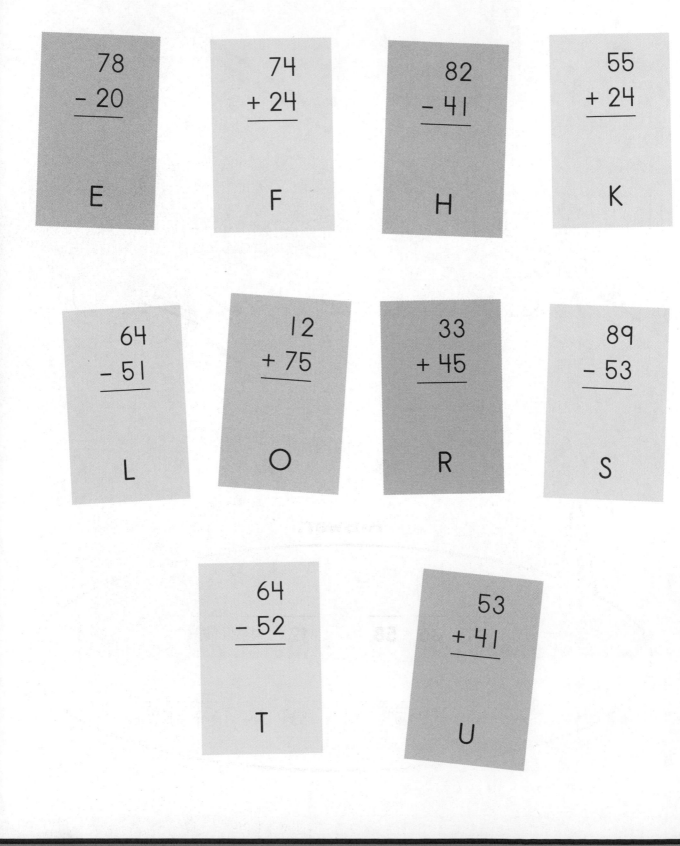

$$\begin{array}{r} 78 \\ -\ 20 \\ \hline \end{array}$$

E

$$\begin{array}{r} 74 \\ +\ 24 \\ \hline \end{array}$$

F

$$\begin{array}{r} 82 \\ -\ 41 \\ \hline \end{array}$$

H

$$\begin{array}{r} 55 \\ +\ 24 \\ \hline \end{array}$$

K

$$\begin{array}{r} 64 \\ -\ 51 \\ \hline \end{array}$$

L

$$\begin{array}{r} 12 \\ +\ 75 \\ \hline \end{array}$$

O

$$\begin{array}{r} 33 \\ +\ 45 \\ \hline \end{array}$$

R

$$\begin{array}{r} 89 \\ -\ 53 \\ \hline \end{array}$$

S

$$\begin{array}{r} 64 \\ -\ 52 \\ \hline \end{array}$$

T

$$\begin{array}{r} 53 \\ +\ 41 \\ \hline \end{array}$$

U

Riddle:

What did Yoda say when Luke tried to eat his dinner with a spoon?

Answer:

$$\frac{}{94} \quad \frac{}{36} \quad \frac{}{58} \qquad \frac{}{12} \quad \frac{}{41} \quad \frac{}{58}$$

$$\frac{}{98} \quad \frac{}{87} \quad \frac{}{78} \quad \frac{}{79} \quad , \qquad \frac{}{13} \quad \frac{}{94} \quad \frac{}{79} \quad \frac{}{58} \quad .$$

Baby Jawa

Add to find the **sums**.

Use your answers to decode the riddle.

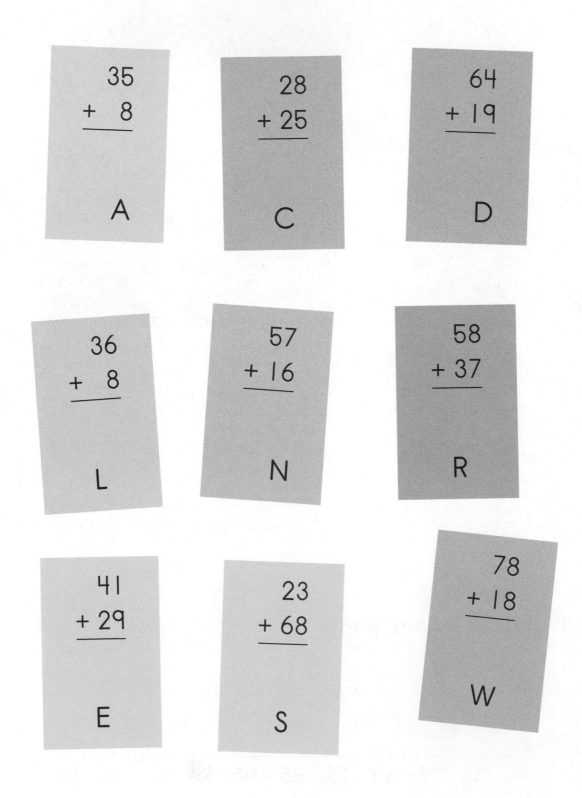

$$35 + 8$$

A

$$28 + 25$$

C

$$64 + 19$$

D

$$36 + 8$$

L

$$57 + 16$$

N

$$58 + 37$$

R

$$41 + 29$$

E

$$23 + 68$$

S

$$78 + 18$$

W

Riddle:

What do you call a baby Jawa?

Answer:

___ ___ ___ ___ ___ ___ ___ ___ ___ ___ ___ ___
43   91 43 73 83 53 95 43 96 44 70 95

Yoda's Garden

Add to find the **sums**.

Use your answers to decode the riddle.

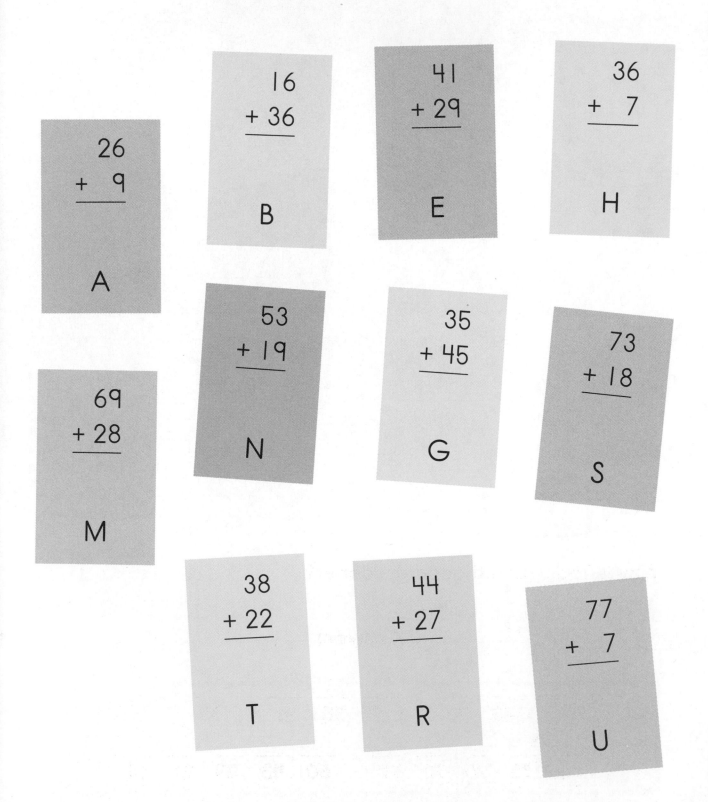

$$26 + 9$$
A

$$16 + 36$$
B

$$41 + 29$$
E

$$36 + 7$$
H

$$53 + 19$$
N

$$35 + 45$$
G

$$73 + 18$$
S

$$69 + 28$$
M

$$38 + 22$$
T

$$44 + 27$$
R

$$77 + 7$$
U

Riddle:

Why is Yoda such a good gardener?

Answer:

	43	70		43	35	91		35	
80	71	70	70	72	60	43	84	97	52

Subtraction Bingo

Subtract to find the **differences**.

Color the cards with answers that match Darth Maul's card.

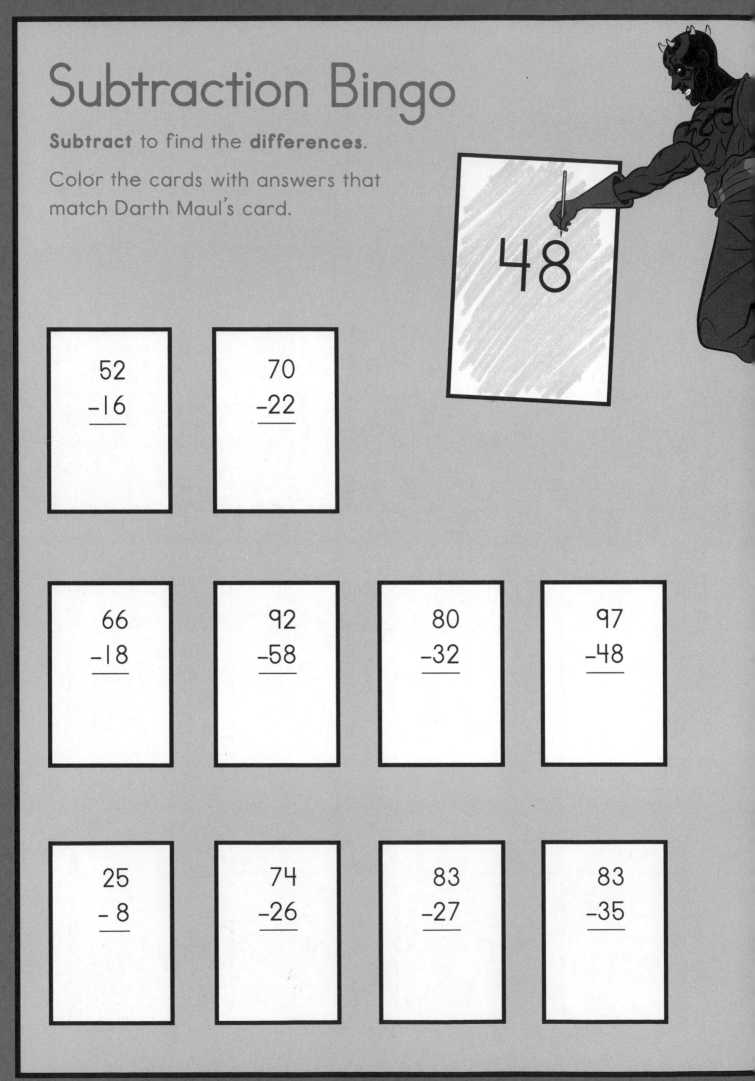

48

52 −16	70 −22

66 −18	92 −58	80 −32	97 −48

25 − 8	74 −26	83 −27	83 −35

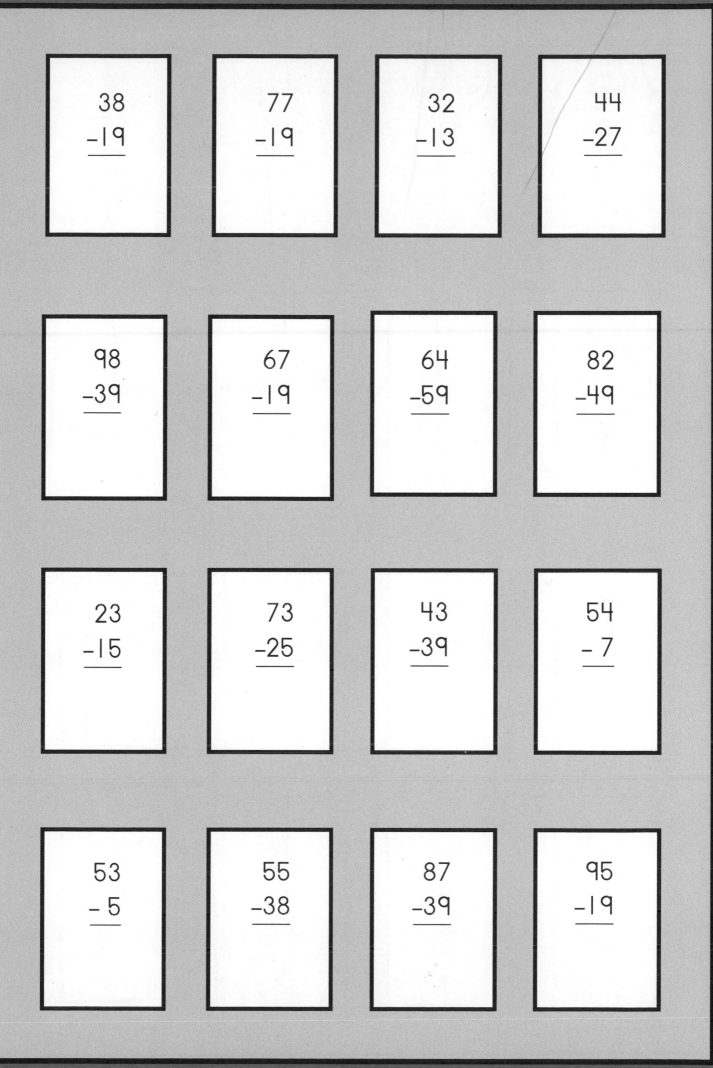

```
  38        77        32        44
 -19       -19       -13       -27
 ___       ___       ___       ___


  98        67        64        82
 -39       -19       -59       -49
 ___       ___       ___       ___


  23        73        43        54
 -15       -25       -39       - 7
 ___       ___       ___       ___


  53        55        87        95
 - 5       -38       -39       -19
 ___       ___       ___       ___
```

Math Matchmaker

Subtract to find the **differences**.

The answer on each card has a matching answer on a second card.

Color each pair of answers with the same color.

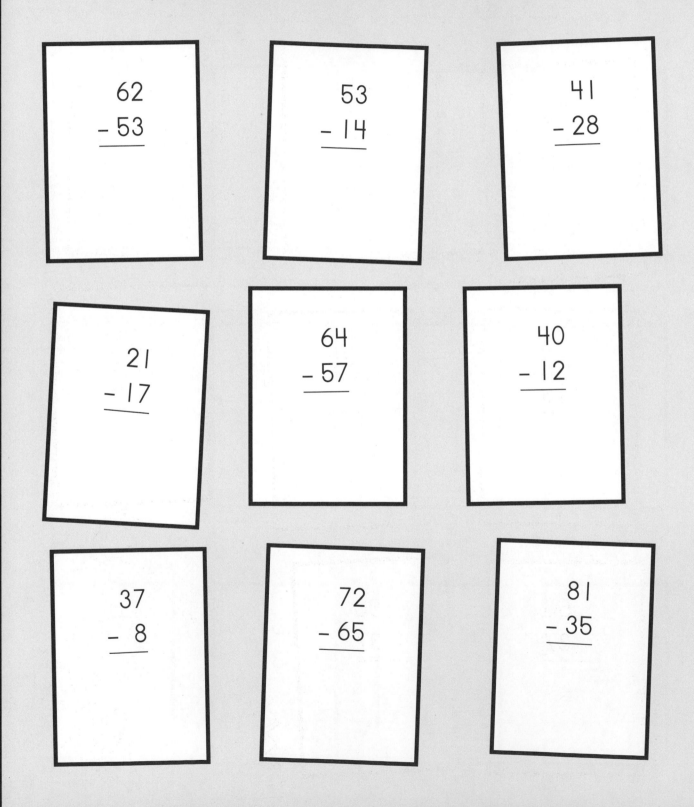

$$62 - 53$$

$$53 - 14$$

$$41 - 28$$

$$21 - 17$$

$$64 - 57$$

$$40 - 12$$

$$37 - 8$$

$$72 - 65$$

$$81 - 35$$

How Many 4s?

Add to find the **sums**.

Color the cards that have 4 ones in the answer.

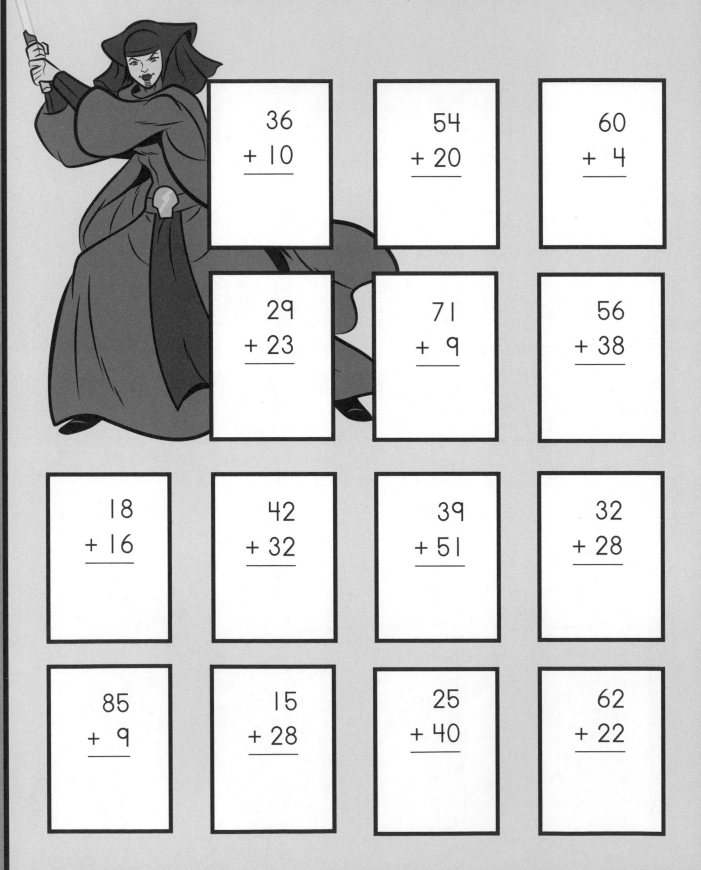

36
+ 10
———

54
+ 20
———

60
+ 4
———

29
+ 23
———

71
+ 9
———

56
+ 38
———

18
+ 16
———

42
+ 32
———

39
+ 51
———

32
+ 28
———

85
+ 9
———

15
+ 28
———

25
+ 40
———

62
+ 22
———

Look for the 9s!

Subtract to find the **differences**.

Color the cards that have 9 ones in the answer.

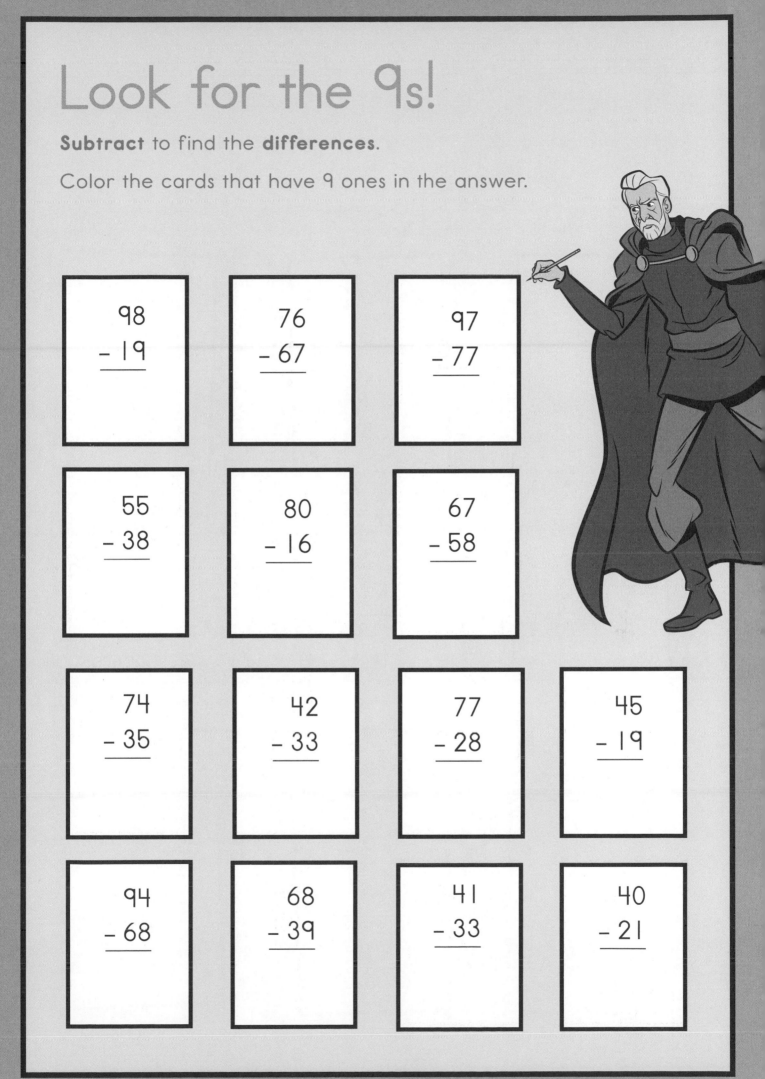

98 − 19	76 − 67	97 − 77
55 − 38	80 − 16	67 − 58

74 − 35	42 − 33	77 − 28	45 − 19
94 − 68	68 − 39	41 − 33	40 − 21

Math Concentration

Add or **subtract**.

Color the two cards on this page that have matching answers.

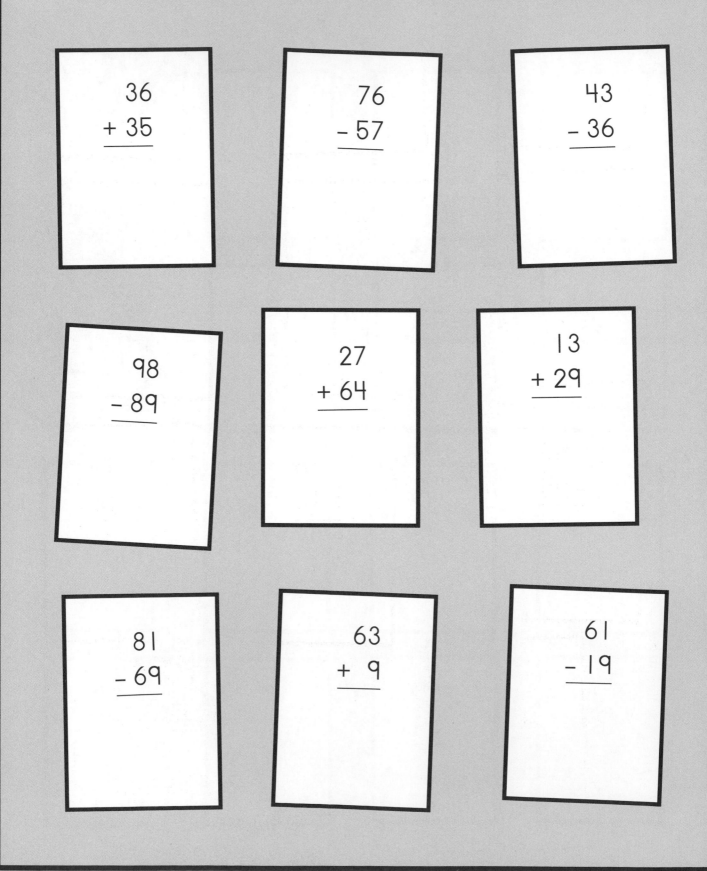

$$36 + 35$$

$$76 - 57$$

$$43 - 36$$

$$98 - 89$$

$$27 + 64$$

$$13 + 29$$

$$81 - 69$$

$$63 + 9$$

$$61 - 19$$

Add or **subtract**.

Color the two cards on this page that have matching answers.

83
− 26

49
+ 13

91
− 56

50
− 33

45
+ 45

14
+ 68

90
− 44

16
+ 18

19
− 16

17
+ 18

Word Problems

Read each word problem.

Decide if you need to **add** or **subtract**.

Write the **number sentence**.

Write the answer in the yellow box.

Han Solo read 25 pages of his book yesterday.

He read 18 pages today.

How many pages did he read in all?

_____

Mace Windu wants to give a lightsaber to every Padawan.

If he has 30 lightsabers and there are 46 Padawans, how many more lightsabers does he need?

_____

15 Jedi are waiting in a line. Obi-Wan Kenobi is tenth in line. How many Jedi are behind Obi-Wan in line?

_____

Luke Skywalker is looking for Darth Vader in starfighters.

He searched 11 X-wings and 13 vulture droids.

How many starfighters did he search altogether?

_____

The band has 4 human musicians and 7 alien musicians.

Does the band have more human musicians or alien musicians?

_____

How many more?

_____

There were 37 sandwiches on a table.

Anakin ate 10 sandwiches, and Padmé ate 4 sandwiches.

How many sandwiches did they eat?

_____

How many sandwiches are left?

_____

Hundreds of Stars

Add to find the **sums.**

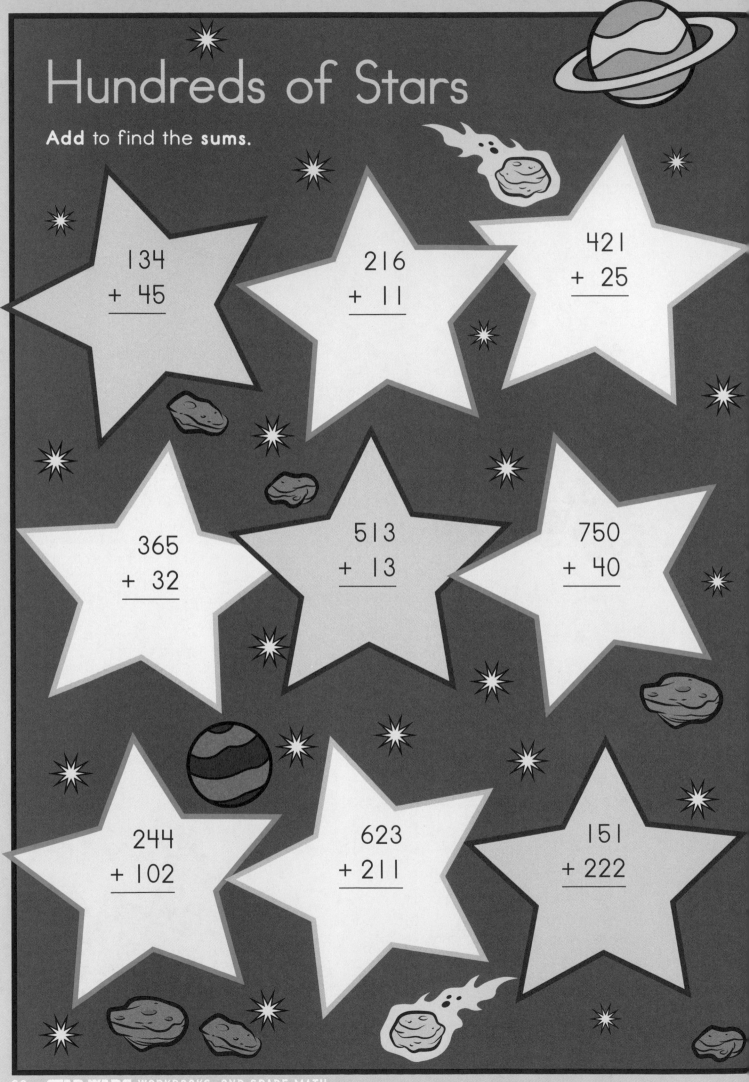

134
+ 45

216
+ 11

421
+ 25

365
+ 32

513
+ 13

750
+ 40

244
+ 102

623
+ 211

151
+ 222

Subtract to find the **differences.**

$$556 - 3$$

$$862 - 11$$

$$688 - 64$$

$$964 - 22$$

$$468 - 51$$

$$759 - 19$$

$$473 - 132$$

$$848 - 212$$

$$287 - 166$$

Math Arrays

An **array** is a set of things arranged into equal groups.

Instead of counting objects one by one, you can put the objects into equal groups and count the groups.

Here is an **array** of 6 Death Stars.

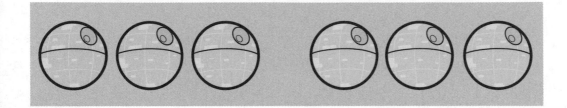

Here is another **array** of 6 Death Stars.

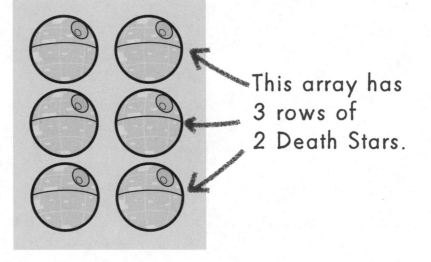

This array has 3 rows of 2 Death Stars.

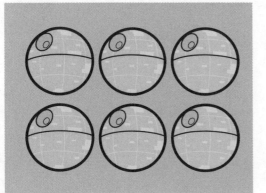

Here is another **array** of 6 Death Stars.

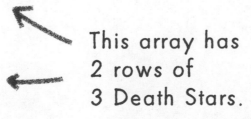

This array has 2 rows of 3 Death Stars.

Here is an **array** of 8 Death Stars.

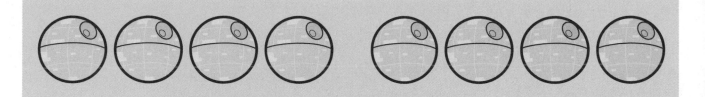

Draw another array of 8 Death Stars.

Can you draw one more array of 8 Death Stars?

Planet Arrays

Here is an **array** of 12 planets.

Draw at least two more arrays for 12 planets.

Here is an **array** of 18 planets.

Draw at least two more arrays for 18 planets.

Repeated Addition

Each of the colored card groupings has the same number of Gungans.

Write how many Gungans and how many cards are in each grouping.

Then write the **repeated addition sentence**.

There are ___4___ Gungans on each card.

There are ___3___ cards.

$$4 + 4 + 4 = 12$$

There are _____ Gungans on each card.

There are _____ cards.

_____

There are _____ Gungans on each card.

There are _____ cards.

_____

There are _____ Gungans on each card.

There are _____ cards.

_____

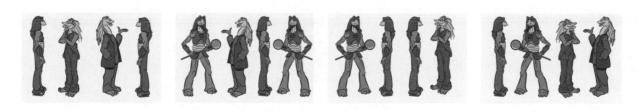

There are _____ Gungans on each card.

There are _____ cards.

_____

Groups of Banthas

Finish the **addition** sentences.

2 + 2 + __2__ + __2__ = __8__

4 + ___ = ___

5   +   ___   +   ___   +   ___   =   ___

6   +   ___   +   ___   =   ___

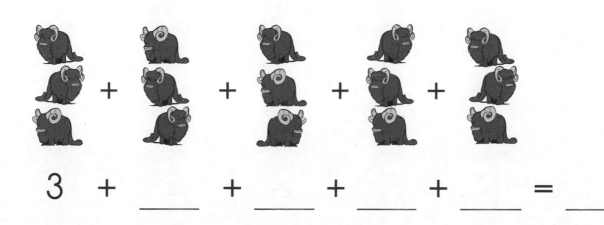

3   +   ___   +   ___   +   ___   +   ___   =   ___

Matching Creatures

Solve each **number sentence**.

The answer on each creature has a matching answer on a second creature.

Color each pair of creatures with the same color.

1 + 1 + 1 + 1 = ____

$$\begin{array}{r} 3 \\ 3 \\ 3 \\ +\ 3 \\ \hline \end{array}$$

8 + 8 = ____

4 + 4 + 4 + 4 = ____

$$\begin{array}{r} 12 \\ +12 \\ \hline \end{array}$$

$$\begin{array}{r} 6 \\ +6 \\ \hline \end{array}$$

$5 + 5 + 5 + 5 + 5 + 5 =$ _____

$8 + 8 + 8 =$ _____

$2 + 2 =$ _____

$10 + 10 + 10 =$ _____

$5 + 5 =$ _____

$2 + 2 + 2 + 2 + 2 =$ _____

Word Problems

Read each word problem. Write the **number sentence** on the line.

Write the answer in the yellow box.

Anakin has 4 bags of droid parts.
There are 6 droid parts in each bag.
How many droid parts does Anakin have?

$$6 + 6 + 6 + 6 = \quad 24$$

Obi-Wan is putting lightsabers into cabinets.
Each cabinet holds 5 lightsabers.
Obi-Wan filled 4 cabinets.
How many lightsabers did he put away?

_____

Padmé is giving 1 robe to each of her 8 handmaidens.
How many robes does Padmé need?

_____

Droids are sold in boxes with 3 droids in each box.
If Luke bought 5 boxes, how many droids did
he buy altogether?

_____

Chewbacca and Han have to paint 6 rooms.
Each room needs 2 cans of paint. How many cans
of paint do they need to do all 6 rooms?

_____

Each dewback needs to drink 2 buckets of
water every day. How many buckets of water
are needed for 4 dewbacks every day?

_____

Aayla Secura can defeat 3 clone troopers every minute.
How many clone troopers can she defeat in 6 minutes?

_____

$\frac{1}{2}$ Is One Half

Fractions show parts of a whole.
They can be written in words (**one half**)
or as a figure ($\frac{1}{2}$).

Color **one half** of each shape.

Write the **fraction** in the space you colored.

How many halves does each shape have? _____

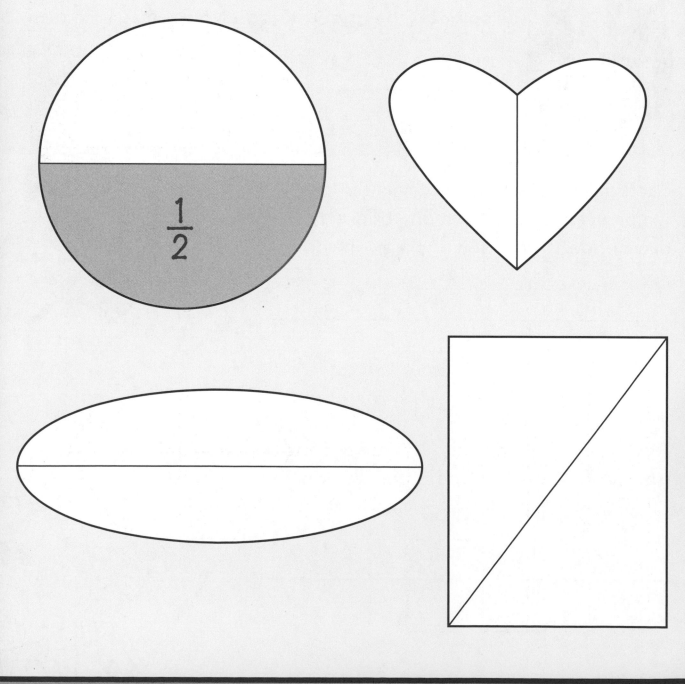

$\frac{1}{4}$ Is One Quarter

Color **one quarter** of each shape.

Write the **fraction** in the space you colored.

How many quarters does each shape have? _____

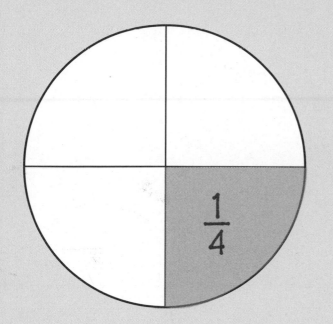

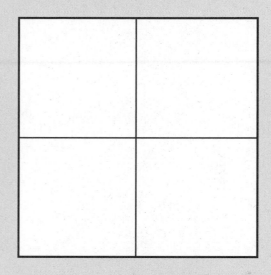

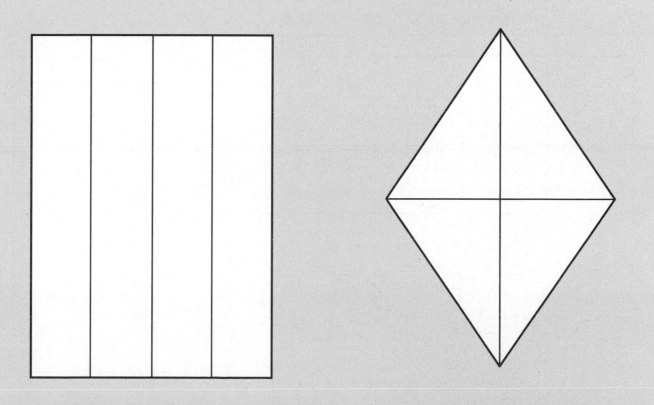

⅓ Is One Third

Color **one third** of each shape.

Write the **fraction** in the space you colored.

How many thirds does each shape have? _____

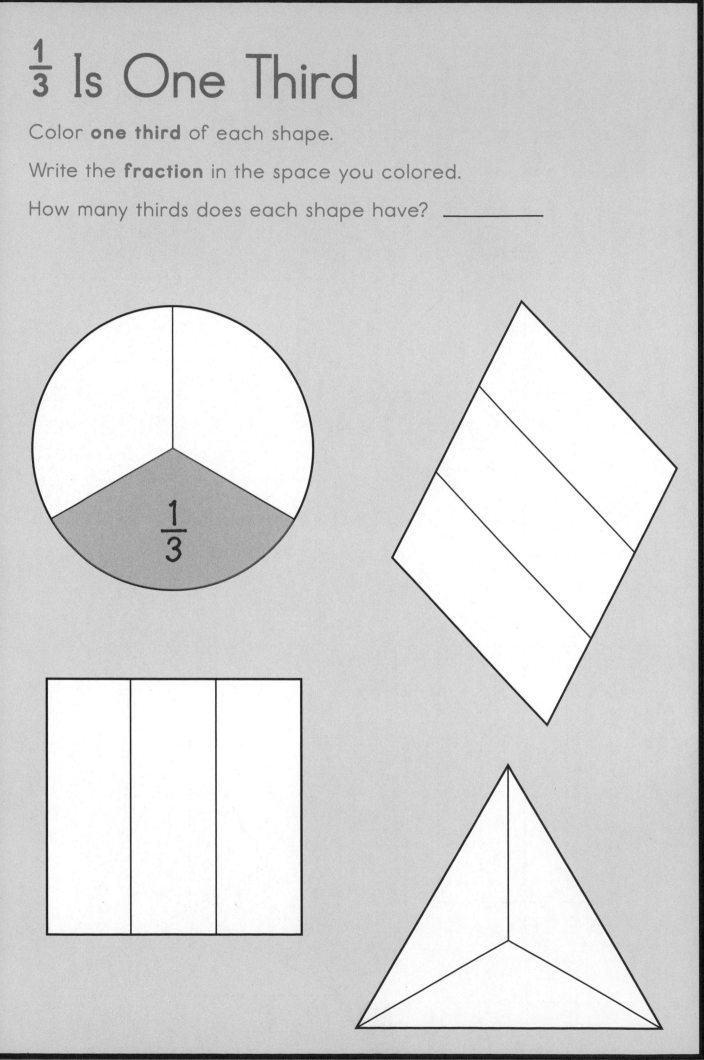

$\frac{1}{3}$

$\frac{1}{6}$ Is One Sixth

Color **one sixth** of each shape.

Write the **fraction** in the space you colored.

How many sixths does each shape have? _____

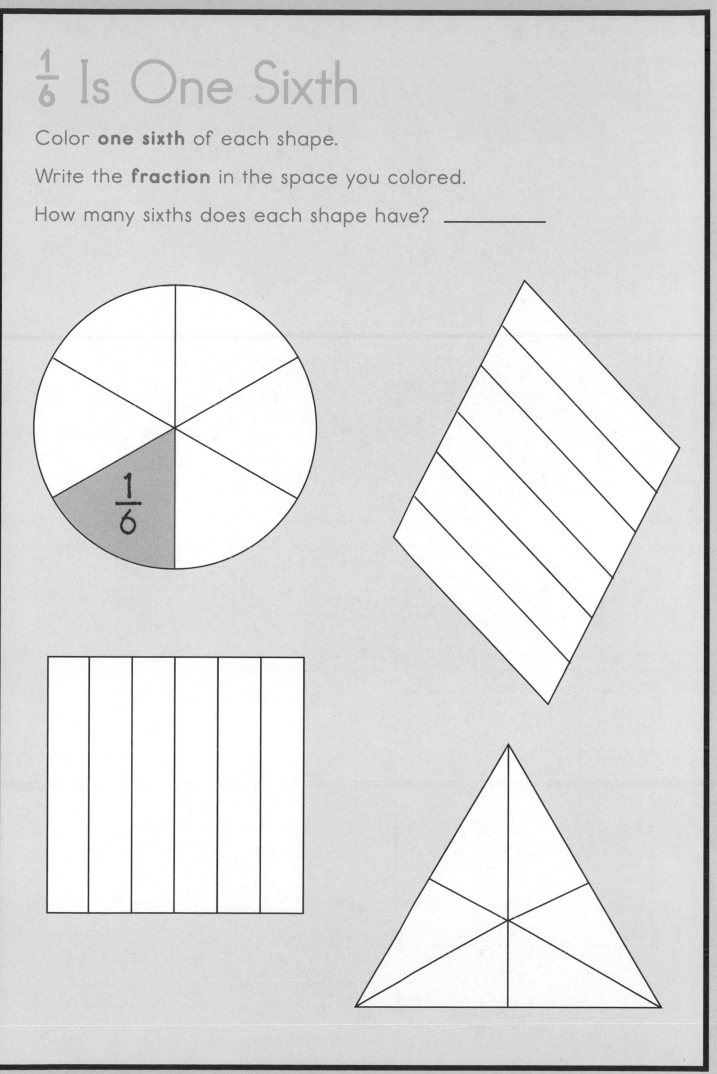

Planetary Fractions

Color in the **fractions**.

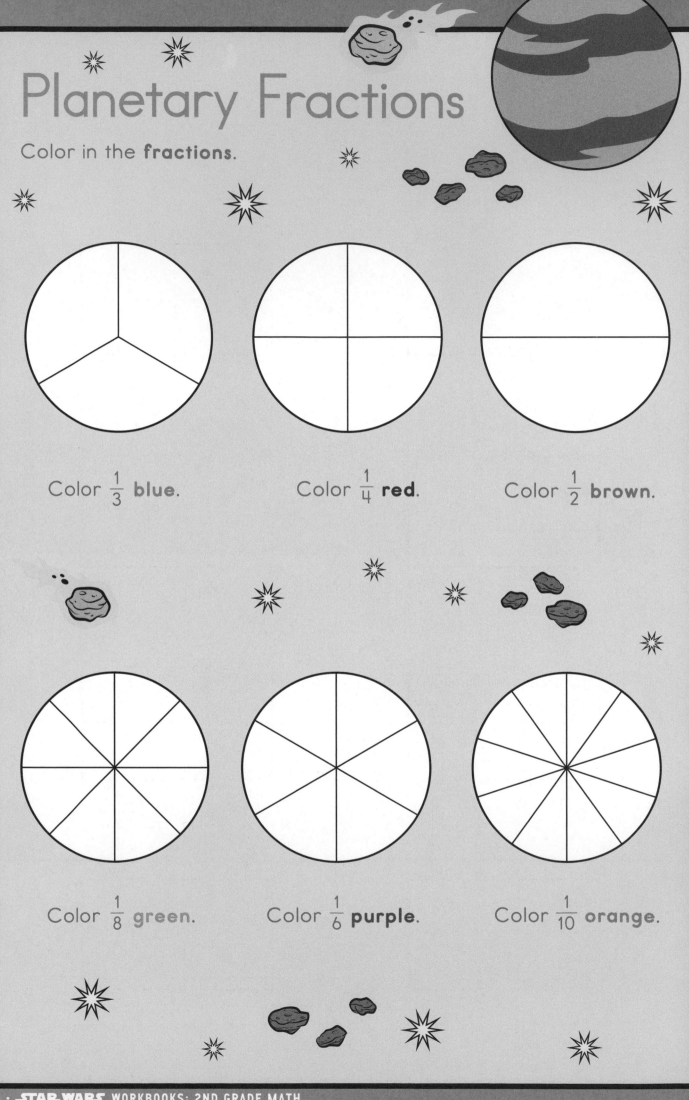

Color $\frac{1}{3}$ **blue**.

Color $\frac{1}{4}$ **red**.

Color $\frac{1}{2}$ **brown**.

Color $\frac{1}{8}$ **green**.

Color $\frac{1}{6}$ **purple**.

Color $\frac{1}{10}$ **orange**.

Matching Fractions

Write the **fraction** on the line.

Draw a line to the **fractions** that are the same.

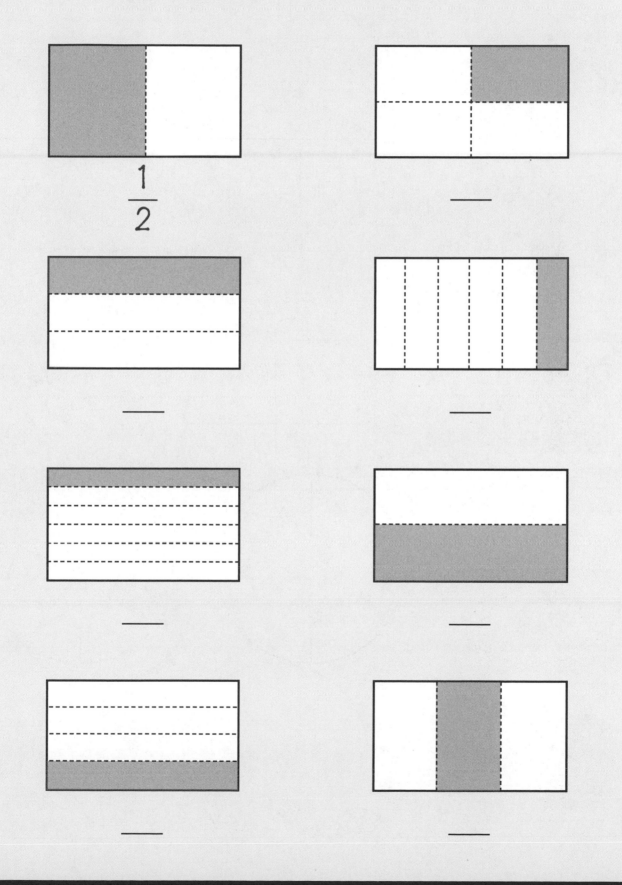

A Piece of Planet

Draw a line from the **fraction** to the matching shape.

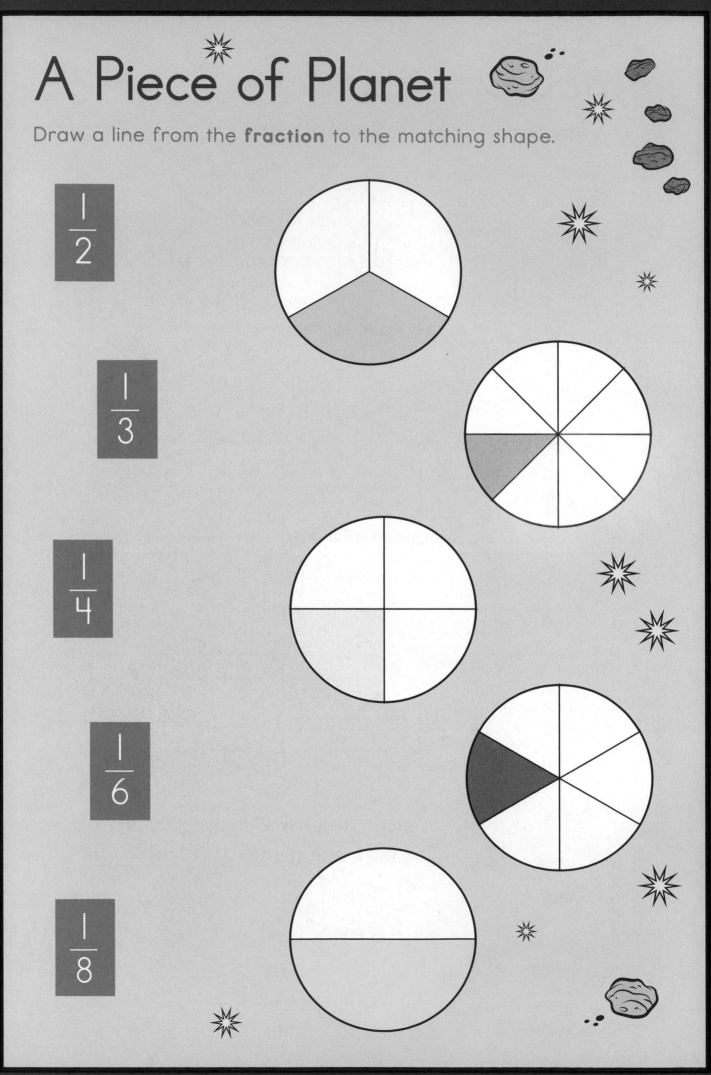

$\frac{1}{2}$

$\frac{1}{3}$

$\frac{1}{4}$

$\frac{1}{6}$

$\frac{1}{8}$

What Fraction?

Read each word problem.
Write the answer in words on the line.
Write the answer as a **fraction** in the box.

Leia cut her apple in half.

If she eats one piece of the apple, how much will she have left to give to Luke?

_____ ☐

Chewbacca cut a sandwich in thirds.

If he eats one piece of the sandwich, what fraction of the sandwich did he eat?

☐

_____

Yoda cuts a pie into four equal pieces.
If he eats one piece of pie, what fraction of the pie did he eat?

☐

_____

Shape Riddles

Read the clues.

Draw a line from the shape to the riddle that matches.

Write the name of the shape on the line.

circle

I have two long sides
and two short sides.

_____

diamond

I have three sides.
I have three angles.

_____

triangle

I have four sides.
All of my sides are the same size.

_____

square

I have four sides.
I look like two triangles stuck together.

_____

rectangle

I have no straight lines.

_____

Same Shape

Look at the shape on each card.

Draw a matching shape on the card next to it.

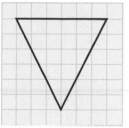

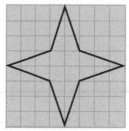

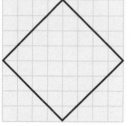
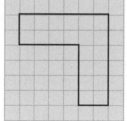

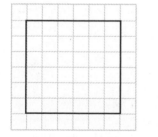
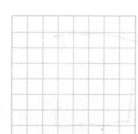
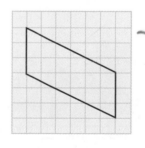

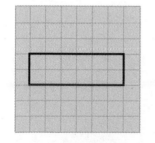
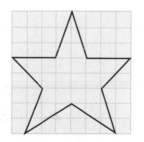

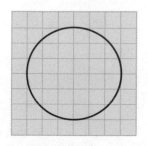

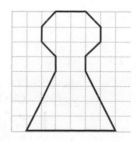

Geometry Riddles

Read the clues.

Draw a line from the 3D shape to the matching riddle.

Write the name of the shape on the line.

cube

I have 1 flat face that is a circle.
I also have 1 curved face.

_____

cone

I have 4 rectangular faces.
I have 2 faces that are squares.

_____

pyramid

I have no straight edges.
I have no flat faces.

_____

box

My base is a square.
My 4 faces are triangles.

_____

sphere

I have 6 square faces.
I have 12 straight edges.

_____

Answers

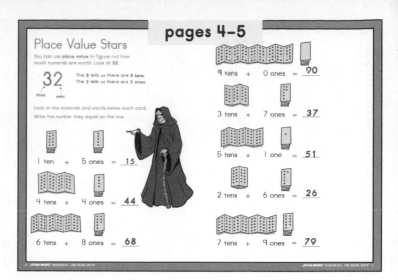

Place Value Stars

You can use **place value** to figure out how much numerals are worth. Look at **32**:

32

The 3 tells us there are **3 tens**.
The 2 tells us there are **2 ones**.

Look at the numerals and words below each card.
Write the number they equal on the line.

1 ten + 5 ones = **15**

4 tens + 4 ones = **44**

6 tens + 8 ones = **68**

9 tens + 0 ones = **90**

3 tens + 7 ones = **37**

5 tens + 1 one = **51**

2 tens + 6 ones = **26**

7 tens + 9 ones = **79**

Hundreds

If you see three numerals, you know that the number is made up of **hundreds, tens,** and **ones.** Look at **642:**

642

The 6 tells us there are 6 hundreds.
The 4 tells us there are 4 tens.
The 2 tells us there are 2 ones.

Circle the correct numeral.

Circle the ones. 56**9**
Circle the tens. **8**
Circle the hundreds. **0**5
Circle the tens. **6**
Circle the hundreds. **6**0
Circle the ones. 5**6**
Circle the hundreds. **0**57
Circle the ones. 91**7**
Circles the tens. **8**

Look at each number.
Then answer the questions.

275 How many hundreds? **2** tens? **7** ones? **5**
481 How many hundreds? **4** tens? **8** ones? **1**
802 How many hundreds? **8** tens? **0** ones? **2**
689 How many hundreds? **6** tens? **8** ones? **9**
743 How many hundreds? **7** tens? **4** ones? **3**
500 How many hundreds? **5** tens? **0** ones? **0**
318 How many hundreds? **3** tens? **1** ones? **8**
957 How many hundreds? **9** tens? **5** ones? **7**
45 How many hundreds? **0** tens? **4** ones? **5**
113 How many hundreds? **1** tens? **1** ones? **3**

More Hundreds

Write the **place value** for each numeral on the chart.

	hundreds	tens	ones
426	4	2	6
193	1	9	3
501	5	0	1
978	9	7	8
345	3	4	5
109	1	0	9
272	2	7	2
486	4	8	6
814	8	1	4
768	7	6	8
659	6	5	9
321	3	2	1

Draw a line to match the words to the number.

6 hundreds, 1 ten, 7 ones — 834
3 hundreds, 2 tens, 8 ones — 173
4 hundreds, 9 tens — 328
2 hundreds, 5 tens, 2 ones — 490
9 hundreds, 1 one — 7
8 hundreds, 3 tens, 4 ones — 617
7 ones — 252
1 hundred, 7 tens, 3 ones — 901

Words to Numbers

Draw a line to match the words to the number.

5 hundreds, 1 ten — 32
8 tens, 8 ones — 285
3 tens, 2 ones — 943
1 hundred, 2 tens, 3 ones — 701
7 hundreds, 1 one — 510
2 hundreds, 8 tens, 5 ones — 123
9 hundreds, 4 tens, 3 ones — 88

Write out the number **529** using words:

Five hundred twenty-nine

...on the sandcrawlers.

forty-seven — 47
twenty-two — 22
one hundred thirty-eight — 138
three hundred twelve — 312
seven hundred eighty-nine — 789
six hundred eighteen — 618
nine hundred two — 902

You're Invited!

The Ewoks are having a party for your birthday! Help them write the invitation by filling in the blanks. Write the numbers in words.

_____ your name
will be _____ age _____ years old on
_____ month _____ day
Where: _____ street address
_____ city _____ state
When: _____ date
At: _____ time

Compare the Candles

Write the number of candles beneath each birthday cake. Then write < or > to show which cake has more candles.
< means less than.
> means greater than.

11 < 14
9 > 6
12 < 15
6 < 12

More or Less?

Write > or < to show which group has more clone troopers.

Comparing Lightsabers

Compare the number of lightsabers.
Write > or < to show which group has more lightsabers.

Write > or < to show which number is greater.

12 < 17   364 > 346
98 < 100   289 > 198
45 < 65   500 < 600
11 < 21   823 < 843
88 > 8   900 > 899
102 < 103   240 < 340

Answers

pages 20–21

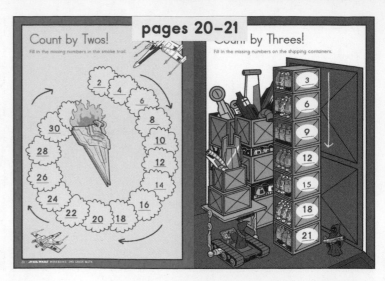

Count by Twos!
Fill in the missing numbers in the smoke trail.

2, 4, 6, 8, 10, 12, 14, 16, 18, 20, 22, 24, 26, 28, 30

Count by Threes!
Fill in the missing numbers on the shipping containers.

3, 6, 9, 12, 15, 18, 21

pages 22–23

Count by Fours!
Fill in the missing numbers in the bubbles.

4, 8, 12, 16, 20, 24, 28, 32, 36, 40

Count by Fives!
Fill in the missing numbers on the flags.

5, 10, 15, 20, 25
30, 35, 40, 45, 50
55, 60, 65, 70, 75
80, 85, 90, 95, 100

pages 24–25

Count by Tens!
Fill in the missing numbers on the droids.

10, 20, 30, 40, 50
60, 70, 80, 90, 100
110, 120, 130, 140, 150
160, 170, 180, 190, 200
210, 220, 230, 240, 250

Count by Hundreds!
Fill in the missing numbers on the planets.

100, 200, 300, 400, 500, 600, 700, 800, 900, 1000

pages 26-27

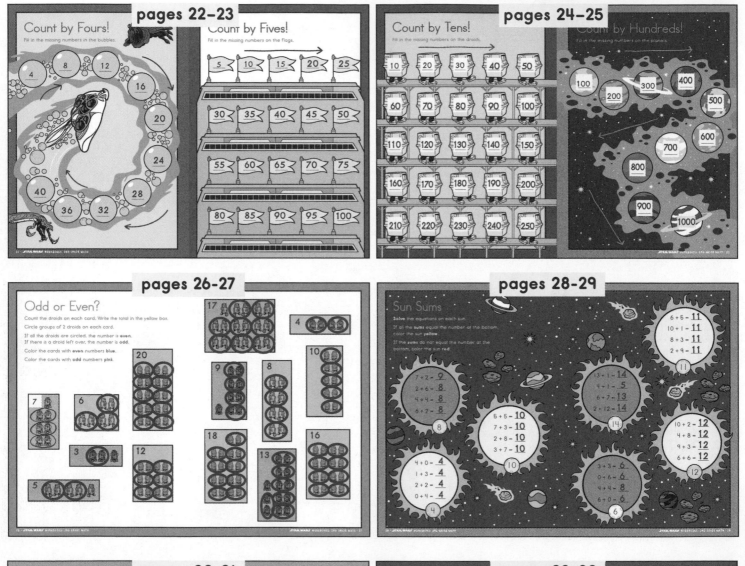

Odd or Even?

Count the droids on each card. Write the total in the yellow box.

Circle groups of 2 droids on each card.

If all the droids are circled, the number is **even**.
If there is a droid left over, the number is **odd**.

Color the cards with **even** numbers **blue**.
Color the cards with **odd** numbers **pink**.

17, 4, 20, 10, 9, 8, 7, 6, 3, 12, 18, 13, 16, 5

pages 28-29

Sun Sums

Solve the equations on each sun.

If all the **sums** equal the number at the bottom, color the sun **yellow**.

If the **sums** do not equal the number at the bottom, color the sun **red**.

$7 + 2 = 9$
$2 + 6 = 8$
$4 + 4 = 8$
$6 + 2 = 8$
8

$6 + 5 = 10$
$7 + 3 = 10$
$2 + 8 = 10$
$3 + 7 = 10$
10

$4 + 0 = 4$
$1 + 3 = 4$
$2 + 2 = 4$
$0 + 4 = 4$
4

$13 + 1 = 14$
$4 + 1 = 5$
$6 + 7 = 13$
$2 + 12 = 14$
14

$3 + 3 = 6$
$0 + 6 = 6$
$4 + 4 = 8$
$6 + 0 = 6$
6

$6 + 5 = 11$
$10 + 1 = 11$
$8 + 3 = 11$
$2 + 9 = 11$
11

$10 + 2 = 12$
$4 + 8 = 12$
$9 + 3 = 12$
$6 + 6 = 12$
12

pages 30-31

Add 10
Add. Write the **sum** on the line.

$6 + 10 = 16$
$10 + 10 = 20$
$56 + 10 = 66$
$33 + 10 = 43$
$900 + 10 = 910$

$124 + 10 = 134$
$157 + 10 = 167$
$235 + 10 = 245$
$868 + 10 = 878$
$544 + 10 = 554$
$667 + 10 = 677$
$212 + 10 = 222$
$345 + 10 = 355$

pages 32-33

Add 100
Add. Write the **sum** on the line.

$100 + 100 = 200$
$139 + 100 = 239$
$236 + 100 = 336$
$445 + 100 = 545$
$685 + 100 = 785$
$899 + 100 = 999$

$711 + 100 = 811$
$600 + 100 = 700$
$533 + 100 = 633$
$406 + 100 = 506$
$871 + 100 = 971$
$395 + 100 = 495$
$319 + 100 = 419$
$800 + 100 = 900$
$668 + 100 = 768$

pages 34–35 · pages 36–37 · pages 38–39 · pages 40–41 · pages 42–43 · pages 44–45 · pages 46–47 · pages 48–49

Answers

pages 50–51

Luke's Dinner

Add or subtract.
Use your answers to decode the riddle.

Riddle:
What did Yoda say when Luke tried to eat his dinner with a spoon?

78 − 20 = **58** E	74 + 24 = **98** F	82 − 41 = **41** H	55 + 24 = **79** K
64 − 51 = **13** L	12 + 75 = **87** O	33 + 45 = **78** R	89 − 53 = **36** S
64 − 52 = **12** T	53 + 41 = **94** U		

Answer:

U S E T H E
94 36 58 12 41 58

F O R K, L U K E.
98 87 78 79 13 94 79 58

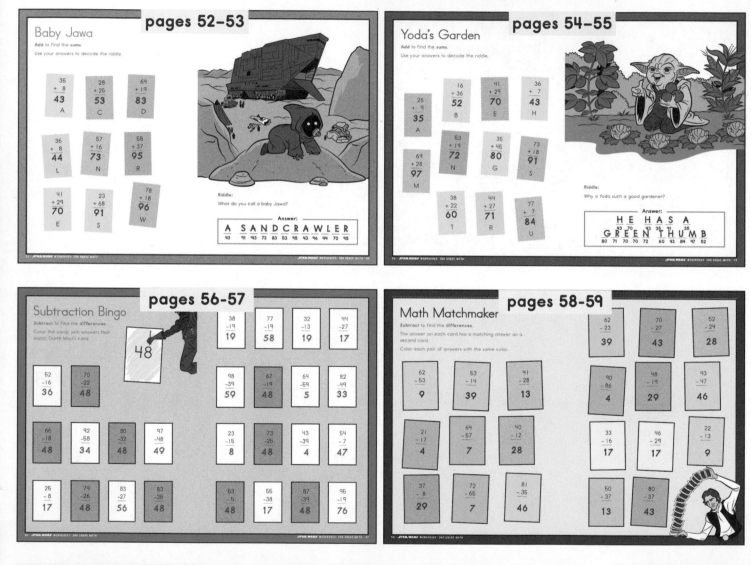

pages 52–53

Baby Jawa

Add to find the sums.
Use your answers to decode the riddle.

35 + 8 = **43** A	28 + 25 = **53** C	64 + 19 = **83** D
36 + 8 = **44** L	57 + 16 = **73** N	58 + 37 = **95** R
41 + 29 = **70** E	23 + 68 = **91** S	78 + 18 = **96** W

Riddle:
What do you call a baby Jawa?

Answer:

A S A N D C R A W L E R
43 91 43 73 83 53 95 43 96 44 70 95

pages 54–55

Yoda's Garden

Add to find the sums.
Use your answers to decode the riddle.

26 + 9 = **35** A	16 + 36 = **52** B	41 + 29 = **70** E	36 + 7 = **43** H
69 + 28 = **97** M	53 + 19 = **72** N	35 + 45 = **80** G	73 + 18 = **91** S
38 + 22 = **60** T	44 + 27 = **71** U	77 + 7 = **84** U	

Riddle:
Why is Yoda such a good gardener?

Answer:

H E H A S A
43 70 43 35 52 35

G R E E N T H U M B
80 71 70 70 72 60 43 84 97 52

pages 56–57

Subtraction Bingo

Subtract to find the differences.
Color the cards with answers that match Darth Maul's card.

48

38 − 19 = **19**	77 − 19 = **58**	32 − 13 = **19**	44 − 27 = **17**
52 − 16 = **36**	70 − 22 = **48**	98 − 39 = **59**	67 − 19 = **48**	64 − 59 = **5**	82 − 49 = **33**
66 − 18 = **48**	92 − 58 = **34**	80 − 32 = **48**	97 − 48 = **49**	23 − 15 = **8**	73 − 25 = **48**	43 − 39 = **4**	54 − 7 = **47**
25 − 8 = **17**	74 − 26 = **48**	83 − 27 = **56**	83 − 35 = **48**	53 − 5 = **48**	55 − 38 = **17**	87 − 39 = **48**	95 − 19 = **76**

pages 58–59

Math Matchmaker

Subtract to find the differences.
The answer on each card has a matching answer on a second card.
Color each pair of answers with the same color.

62 − 53 = **9**	53 − 14 = **39**	41 − 28 = **13**	62 − 23 = **39**	70 − 27 = **43**	52 − 24 = **28**
21 − 17 = **?**	64 − 57 = **7**	40 − 12 = **28**	90 − 86 = **4**	61 − 19 = **29**	93 − 47 = **46**
37 − 8 = **29**	72 − 65 = **7**	81 − 35 = **46**	33 − 16 = **17**	46 − 29 = **17**	22 − 13 = **9**
			50 − 37 = **13**	80 − 37 = **43**	

pages 60–61

How Many 4s?

Add to find the sums.
Color the cards that have 4 ones in the answer.

36 + 10 = **46**	64 + 20 = **74**	60 + 4 = **64**
29 + 23 = **52**	71 + 9 = **80**	56 + 38 = **94**
18 + 16 = **34**	42 + 32 = **74**	39 + 51 = **90**	32 + 28 = **60**
85 + 9 = **94**	15 + 28 = **43**	25 + 40 = **65**	62 + 22 = **84**

Look for the 9s!

Subtract to find the differences.
Color the cards that have 9 ones in the answer.

98 − 19 = **79**	76 − 67 = **9**	97 − 77 = **20**
55 − 38 = **17**	80 − 16 = **64**	67 − 58 = **9**
74 − 35 = **39**	42 − 33 = **9**	77 − 28 = **49**	45 − 19 = **?**
94 − 68 = **26**	68 − 39 = **?**	41 − 33 = **?**	40 − 21 = **19**

pages 62–63

Math Concentration

Add or subtract.
Color the two cards on this page that have matching answers.

36 + 35 = **71**	76 − 57 = **19**	43 − 36 = **7**
98 − 89 = **9**	27 + 64 = **91**	13 + 29 = **42**
81 − 69 = **12**	63 + 9 = **72**	61 − 19 = **42**

Add or subtract.
Color the two cards on this page that have matching answers.

83 − 26 = **57**	49 + 13 = **62**	91 − 56 = **35**
50 − 33 = **17**	45 + 45 = **90**	14 + 68 = **82**
90 − 44 = **46**	16 + 18 = **34**	19 − 16 = **3**
17 + 18 = **35**		

pages 64-65

Word Problems

Read each word problem.
Decide if you need to **add** or **subtract**.
Write the number sentence.
Write the answer in the yellow box.

Han Solo read 25 pages of his book yesterday.
He read 18 pages today.
How many pages did he read in all?

$$25 + 18 = 43$$

Mace Windu wants to give a lightsaber to every Padawan.
If he has 30 lightsabers and there are 46 Padawans, how many more lightsabers does he need?

$$46 - 30 = 16$$

15 Jedi are waiting in a line. Obi-Wan Kenobi is tenth in line. How many Jedi are behind Obi-Wan in line?

$$15 - 10 = 5$$

Luke Skywalker is looking for Darth Vader in starfighters.
He searched 11 X-wings and 13 vulture droids.
How many starfighters did he search altogether?

$$11 + 13 = 24$$

The band has 4 human musicians and 7 alien musicians.
Does the band have more human musicians or alien musicians?

alien musicians

How many more?

$$7 - 4 = 3$$

There were 37 sandwiches on a table.
Anakin ate 10 sandwiches, and Padmé ate 4 sandwiches.
How many sandwiches did they eat?

$$10 + 4 = 14$$

How many sandwiches are left?

$$37 - 14 = 23$$

pages 66-67

Hundreds of Stars

Add to find the sums. Subtract to find the differences.

$$\begin{array}{r}134\\+\ 45\\\hline 179\end{array}\qquad\begin{array}{r}216\\+\ 11\\\hline 227\end{array}\qquad\begin{array}{r}421\\+\ 25\\\hline 446\end{array}$$

$$\begin{array}{r}556\\-\ \ 3\\\hline 553\end{array}\qquad\begin{array}{r}862\\-\ 11\\\hline 851\end{array}\qquad\begin{array}{r}688\\-\ 64\\\hline 624\end{array}$$

$$\begin{array}{r}365\\+\ 32\\\hline 397\end{array}\qquad\begin{array}{r}513\\+\ 13\\\hline 526\end{array}\qquad\begin{array}{r}750\\+\ 40\\\hline 790\end{array}$$

$$\begin{array}{r}964\\-\ 22\\\hline 942\end{array}\qquad\begin{array}{r}468\\-\ 51\\\hline 417\end{array}\qquad\begin{array}{r}759\\-\ 19\\\hline 740\end{array}$$

$$\begin{array}{r}244\\+\ 102\\\hline 346\end{array}\qquad\begin{array}{r}623\\+\ 211\\\hline 834\end{array}\qquad\begin{array}{r}151\\+\ 222\\\hline 373\end{array}$$

$$\begin{array}{r}470\\-\ 132\\\hline 341\end{array}\qquad\begin{array}{r}010\\-\ 212\\\hline 636\end{array}\qquad\begin{array}{r}287\\-\ 166\\\hline 121\end{array}$$

pages 68-69

Math Arrays

An **array** is a set of things arranged into equal groups.
Instead of counting objects one by one, you can put the objects into equal groups and count the groups.

Here is an **array** of 6 Death Stars.

Here is another **array** of 6 Death Stars.

This array has 3 rows of 2 Death Stars.

Here is another **array** of 6 Death Stars.

This array has 2 rows of 3 Death Stars.

Here is an **array** of 8 Death Stars.

Draw another array of 8 Death Stars.

Can you draw one more array of 8 Death Stars?

pages 70-71

Planet Arrays

Here is an **array** of 12 planets.

Draw at least two more arrays for 12 planets.

Here is an **array** of 18 planets.

Draw at least two more arrays for 18 planets.

pages 72-73

Repeated Addition

Each of the colored card groupings has the same number of Gungans.
Write how many Gungans and how many cards are in each grouping.
Then write the **repeated addition sentence**.

There are __4__ Gungans on each card.
There are __3__ cards.

$$4 + 4 + 4 = 12$$

There are __2__ Gungans on each card.
There are __4__ cards.

$$2 + 2 + 2 + 2 = 8$$

There are __3__ Gungans on each card.
There are __3__ cards.

$$3 + 3 + 3 = 9$$

There are __5__ Gungans on each card.
There are __4__ cards.

$$5 + 5 + 5 + 5 = 20$$

There are __4__ Gungans on each card.
There are __4__ cards.

$$4 + 4 + 4 + 4 = 16$$

pages 74-75

Groups of Banthas

Finish the **addition** sentences.

$$2 + 2 + \underline{2} + \underline{2} = \underline{8}$$

$$6 + \underline{6} + \underline{6} = \underline{18}$$

$$4 + \underline{4} = \underline{8}$$

$$5 + \underline{5} + \underline{5} + \underline{5} = \underline{20}$$

$$3 + \underline{3} + \underline{3} + \underline{3} + \underline{3} = \underline{15}$$

pages 76-77

Matching Creatures

Solve each **number sentence**.
The answer on each creature has a matching answer on a second creature.
Color each pair of creatures with the same color.

$$5+5+5+5+5+5=30$$

$$\begin{array}{r}3\\3\\3\\+\ 3\\\hline 12\end{array}$$

$$1+1+1+1=4$$

$$8+8+8=24$$

$$4+4+4+4=16$$

$$\begin{array}{r}8\\+\ 8\\\hline 16\end{array}$$

$$10+10+10=30$$

$$2+2+2+2=8$$

$$\begin{array}{r}12\\+\ 12\\\hline 24\end{array}$$

$$\begin{array}{r}6\\+\ 6\\\hline 12\end{array}$$

$$6+5=10$$

$$2+2+2+2+2=10$$

pages 78-79

Word Problems

Read each word problem. Write the **number sentence** on the line.
Write the answer in the yellow box.

Anakin has 4 bags of droid parts.
There are 6 droid parts in each bag.
How many droid parts does Anakin have?

$$6 + 6 + 6 + 6 = 24$$

Obi-Wan is putting lightsabers into cabinets.
Each cabinet holds 5 lightsabers.
Obi-Wan filled 4 cabinets.
How many lightsabers did he put away?

$$5 + 5 + 5 + 5 = 20$$

Padmé is giving 1 robe to each of her 8 handmaidens.
How many robes does Padmé need?

$$1+1+1+1+1+1+1+1= 8$$

Droids are sold in boxes with 3 droids in each box.
If Luke bought 5 boxes, how many droids did he buy altogether?

$$3+3+3+3+3 = 15$$

Chewbacca and Han have to paint 6 rooms.
Each room needs 2 cans of paint. How many cans of paint do they need to do all 6 rooms?

$$2+2+2+2+2+2= 12$$

Each dewback needs to drink 2 buckets of water every day. How many buckets of water are needed for 4 dewbacks every day?

$$2 + 2 + 2 + 2 = 8$$

Aayla Secura can defeat 3 clone troopers every minute. How many clone troopers can she defeat in 6 minutes?

$$3+3+3+3+3+3 = 18$$

Answers

pages 80–81

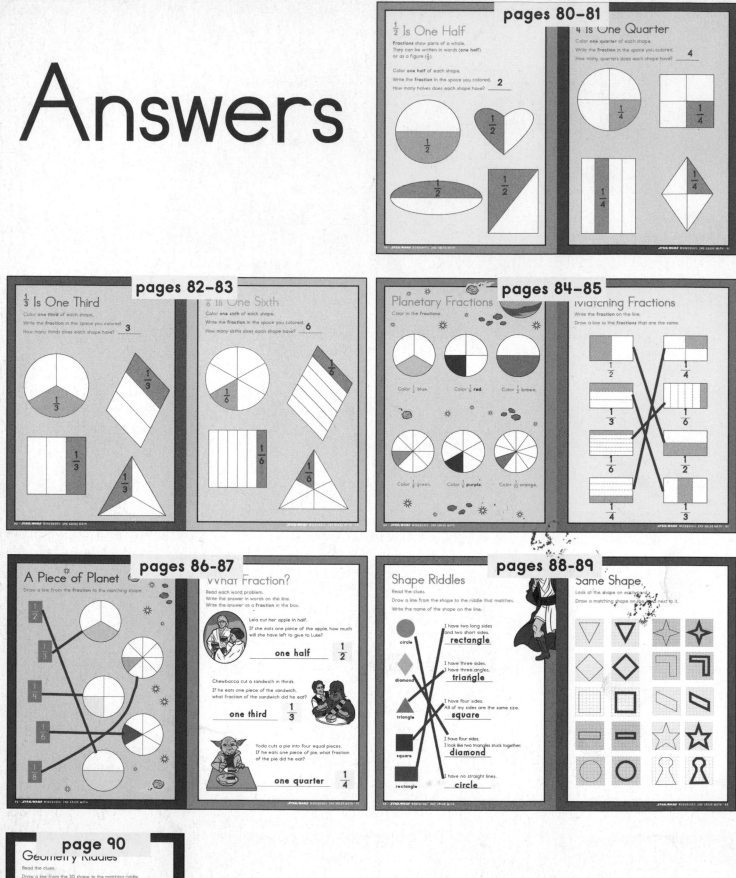

pages 82–83

pages 84–85

pages 86–87

pages 88–89

page 90

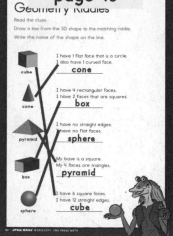